The Atmosphere and Beyond

The Nature of Science S2

Using Weather Data D2

Looking at the Universe D44

HOUGHTON MIFFLIN

BOSTON

Copyright © 2009 by Houghton Mifflin Company. All rights reserved.

Printed in the U.S.A.   ISBN-13: 978-0-547-06253-2   ISBN-10: 0-547-06253-2   4 5 6 7 8 9 0914 16 15 14 13 12 11
4500278491

Do What Scientists Do

Meet Dr. Kenneth Sulak. He works for the United States Geological Survey. He studies fish and other animals that live deep in the ocean. Dr. Sulak wants to find out what kinds of animals live far below the surface. He wants to know how many of them there are and how they live. He also wants to know how deep-sea animals interact with animals in the shallower water above them.

Dr. Sulak's research depends on submersibles. A ship with a crane lowers a sub into the Gulf of Mexico. In it, Dr. Sulak can travel far below the surface to observe and collect deep-sea life.

HARBOR BRANCH
OCEANOGRAPHIC

Ocean fishing, exploring for oil, and other human activities are moving into deeper and deeper water. Dr. Sulak helps keep track of how these activities affect deep-sea life. He shares what he learns by speaking to and answering the questions of other scientists. He also writes about it in science magazines.

Scientists investigate in different ways.

The ways scientists investigate depend on the questions they ask. Dr. Sulak observes animals in their natural habitats. He also classifies animals. Often, he measures water temperatures. Other scientists ask questions that can be answered by doing a fair test called an experiment.

Dr. Kenneth Sulak uses a microscope to learn more about deep-sea life. He has been surprised to discover how many animals live very deep in the ocean and that many deep-sea animals are bright red.

Think Like a Scientist

The ways scientists ask and answer questions about the world around them is called **scientific inquiry.** Scientific inquiry requires certain attitudes, or ways of thinking. To think like a scientist you have to be:

- curious and ask a lot of questions.

- creative and think up new ways to do things.

- able to keep an open mind. That means you listen to the ideas of others.

- open to changing what you think when your investigation results surprise you.

- willing to question what other people tell you.

Tides are changes in the level of the ocean that occur each day. What causes tides?

Use Critical Thinking

When you think critically you make decisions about what others tell you or what you read. Is what you heard or read fact or opinion? A *fact* can be checked to make sure it is true. An *opinion* is what you think about the facts.

Did anyone ever tell you how something works that you found hard to believe? When you ask, "What facts back up your idea?" you are thinking critically. Critical thinkers question scientific statements.

Tides seem to rise and fall at about the same time each day. I wonder what causes tides to keep changing that way?

I read that tides are caused by the pull of the Moon's gravity on Earth's oceans. The level of the oceans keeps rising and falling as the Moon and Earth move into different positions.

Science Inquiry

Using scientific inquiry helps you understand the world around you. For example, suppose you collect a sample of water from the ocean and put it in the freezer over night.

Observe The next day, you notice that the ocean water is not completely frozen. You also notice that ice cubes in the freezer are frozen solid.

Ask a Question When you think about what you saw, heard, or read, you may have questions.

Hypothesis Think about facts you already know. Do you have an idea about the answer? Write it down. That is your hypothesis.

Experiment Plan a test that will tell if the hypothesis is true or not. List the materials and tools you will need. Write the steps you will follow. Make sure that you keep all conditions the same except the one you are testing. That condition is called the *variable.*

Conclusion What do your results tell you? Do they support your hypothesis or show it to be false?

Describe your experiment with enough detail that others can repeat it. Communicate your results and conclusion.

My Salt Water Experiment

Observe It seems that ocean water does not freeze at the same temperature as plain water. Ocean water is salty.

Ask a question How does salt affect the freezing point of water?

Hypothesis Plain water will freeze before salt water because it has a higher freezing point than salt water.

Experiment I will put labeled containers of the same amount of salt water and plain water in a freezer. I will check on the containers every 3 minutes. I will record in which container the water freezes first.

Conclusion Plain water turns to ice before salt water. The results support my hypothesis. Plain water has a higher freezing point than salt water.

Inquiry Process

Here is a process that some scientists follow to answer questions and make new discoveries.

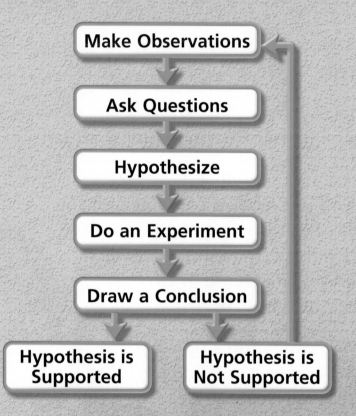

Make Observations

Ask Questions

Hypothesize

Do an Experiment

Draw a Conclusion

Hypothesis is Supported

Hypothesis is Not Supported

Science Inquiry Skills

You'll use many of these inquiry skills when you investigate and experiment.

- Ask Questions
- Observe
- Compare
- Classify
- Predict
- Measure

- Hypothesize
- Use Variables
- Experiment
- Use Models
- Communicate
- Use Numbers

- Record Data
- Analyze Data
- Infer
- Collaborate
- Research

Try It Yourself!

Experiment With an Energy Sphere

When you touch both metal strips of the Energy Sphere, the sphere lights. This works with two people—as long as they are in contact with one another.

1 What questions do you have about the Energy Sphere?

2 How would you find out the answers?

3 Write your experiment plan and predict what will happen.

Be an Inventor

Alberto Behar's interest in space led him to a career in space engineering. Dr. Behar helped to invent a new kind of Martian rover. Called the tumbleweed, it looks more like a giant beach ball than a vehicle. It moves when the wind blows it.

The idea for the tumbleweed came about by accident. During a test of a rover with large inflatable wheels, one of the wheels fell off. The wind blew the wheel several kilometers before someone caught it. The idea of a wind-blown rover was born.

The tumbleweed has performed very well in tests on Earth. Dr. Behar thinks it may soon be used to explore the surface of Mars.

"When I was about seven or eight, I wanted to be an astronaut. I checked out all of the books on space I could at the library..."

What Is Technology?

The tools people make and the things they build with tools are all **technology.** A toy car is technology. So is a race car.

Scientists use technology, too. For example, a laser beam can be used to make very precise measurements. Scientists also use microscopes to see things they cannot see with just their eyes.

Many technologies make the world a better place to live. But sometimes a technology that solves one problem can cause other problems. For example, farmers use fertilizer to increase the yields of their crops. But fertilizer can be carried by rain water into lakes and streams where it can harm fish and other living things.

A Better Idea

"I wish I had a better way to _____." How would you fill in the blank? Everyone wishes they could find a way to do their jobs more easily or have more fun. Inventors try to make those wishes come true. Inventing or improving an invention requires time and patience.

George Hansburg patented the pogo stick in 1919. It was a Y-shaped metal stick with two foot rests and a spring. Today's pogo sticks are not much different.

Pogo Stick

spring

foot rest

How to Be an Inventor

1. **Identify a problem.** It may be a problem at school, at home, or in your community.

2. **List ways to solve the problem.** Sometimes the solution is a new tool. Other times it may be a new way of doing an old job or activity.

3. **Choose the best solution.** Decide which idea you predict will work best. Think about which one you can carry out.

4. **Make a sample.** A sample, called a *prototype,* is the first try. Your idea may need many materials or none at all. Choose measuring tools that will help your design work better.

5. **Try out your invention.** Use your prototype, or ask someone else to try it. Keep a record of how it works and what problems you find. The more times you try it, the more information you will have.

6. **Improve your invention.** Use what you learned to make your design work better. Draw or write about the changes you make and why you made them.

7. **Share your invention.** Show your invention to others. Explain how it works. Tell how it makes an activity easier or more fun. If it did not work as well as you wanted, tell why.

Make Decisions

Trouble for the Everglades

For many years, the water of the Florida Everglades has had too much phosphorus. The phosphorus comes from nearby farms and cities. Phosphorus in fertilizers washes into streams and rivers. Phosphorus in laundry detergents washes down drains. Much of the phosphorus ends up in the water of the Everglades.

Some types of plants and animals have not been able to stand the high phosphorus levels. They have decreased in numbers or even gone extinct. Scientists are trying to reduce the amount of phosphorus entering the Everglades. They are also looking for ways to remove the phosphorus that is already there.

Deciding What to Do

What methods are best to help lower phosphorus levels in the water of the Everglades?

Here's how to make your decision about the phosphorus problem. You can use the same steps to help solve problems in your home, in your school, and in your community.

 **Learn** → Learn about the problem. Take the time needed to get the facts. You could talk to an expert, read a science book, or explore a web site.

List → Make a list of actions you could take. Add actions other people could take.

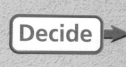 **Decide** → Think about each action on your list. Decide which choice is the best one for you or your community.

Share → Communicate your decision to others.

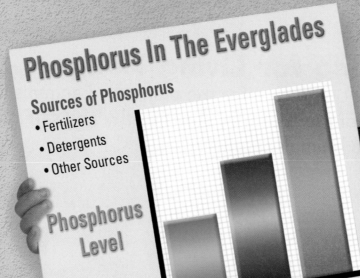

Phosphorus In The Everglades

Sources of Phosphorus
- Fertilizers
- Detergents
- Other Sources

Phosphorus Level

Solutions

Year

Science Safety

☑ Know the safety rules of your school and classroom and follow them.

☑ Read and follow the safety tips in each Investigation activity.

☑ When you plan your own investigations, write down how to keep safe.

☑ Know how to clean up and put away science materials. Keep your work area clean and tell your teacher about spills right away.

☑ Know how to safely plug in electrical devices.

☑ Wear safety goggles when your teacher tells you.

☑ Unless your teacher tells you to, never put any science materials in or near your ears, eyes, or mouth.

☑ Wear gloves when handling live animals.

☑ Wash your hands when your investigation is done.

Caring for Living Things

☑ Learn how to care for the plants and animals in your classroom so that they stay healthy and safe. Learn how to hold animals carefully.

The Atmosphere and Beyond

Cricket Connection

Visit www.eduplace.com/scp/ to check out *Click, Ask,* and *Odyssey* magazine articles and activities.

The Atmosphere and Beyond

Chapter 10
Using Weather Data D2

Chapter 11
Looking at the Universe D44

Independent Reading

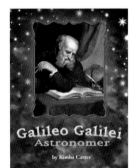

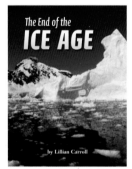

Galileo Galilei Astronomer

Space Animals

The End of the Ice Age

Discover!

In a time-lapse photo, the stars appear to move across the sky in a circular path—except for one star. Which star is the only one that doesn't appear to change its position in the sky? You will have the answer to this question by the end of the unit.

Chapter 10

Using Weather Data

LESSON

1

Planes fly through it and clouds float in it—how does the Earth's atmosphere support life?

Read about it in Lesson 1.

LESSON

2

From clouds to rain to water vapor—how does Earth's water change form?

Read about it in Lesson 2.

LESSON

3

A warm, sunny day with gentle breezes becomes a fierce hurricane with harsh winds—what causes weather to change?

Read about it in Lesson 3.

LESSON

4

Sunny tropical lands and snow-covered poles—what factors cause climates to differ?

Read about it in Lesson 4.

What Is Air?

Why It Matters...

Imagine what it would be like to float among the clouds. Parachutes allow people to drift with the wind and float down from the sky. Air catches inside the parachute and slows the person's fall. Birds and airplanes both need air to fly.

PREPARE TO INVESTIGATE

Inquiry Skill

Compare When you compare two things, you observe how they are alike and how they are different.

Materials

- dowel
- piece of string
- 2 balloons
- tape
- marker
- metric ruler

Balancing Air

Procedure

① **Collaborate** Work with a partner. Tie a string around the center of a dowel. Hold the string while your partner slides the knot along the dowel. The dowel should be balanced so that it stays exactly level.

② **Experiment** Use a metric ruler to help you. Tape two deflated balloons exactly the same distance from the center of the dowel. Slide the knot of the string until the dowel is balanced.

③ **Predict** Use a pencil to mark the dowel at the exact place where one balloon is attached. Then remove that balloon and blow it up. Tie a knot in the neck so that no air escapes. Predict what will happen when you reattach the balloon to the dowel.

④ **Compare** Reattach the balloon to the dowel at the marked place. Compare how the dowel balanced before and after you inflated the balloon.

⑤ **Record Data** Record your observations in your *Science Notebook*.

Conclusion

1. **Compare** Which weighs more, an inflated balloon or a deflated balloon?

2. **Hypothesize** Write a hypothesis about what caused the change in the way the dowel balanced.

STEP 2

STEP 3

STEP 4

Investigate More!

Design an Experiment Find out how much salt you would need to put inside the deflated balloon to balance the dowel. What conclusion can you make about the weight of the air and the weight of the salt?

The Atmosphere

VOCABULARY

air pressure	p. D8
atmosphere	p. D8
greenhouse effect	p. D10
weather	p. D9

READING SKILL

Text Structure Make an outline of the lesson using the headings. Where will you find the answer to the question, What are the layers of the atmosphere?

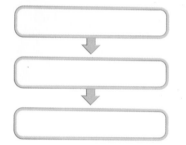

MAIN IDEA The Earth is surrounded by a layer of air that is made up of different gases. These gases are important to Earth's living things.

Gases in Air

Did you ever wonder what is in the air you breathe? Air is a mixture of colorless, odorless gases that surrounds Earth. Nitrogen (NY truh juhn) makes up the largest portion of air. Plants need nitrogen to grow. Oxygen (AHK sih juhn) is the second most common gas in air. Living things need oxygen to survive. Your body needs oxygen to use the energy in the food you eat. Most living things get the oxygen they need from air.

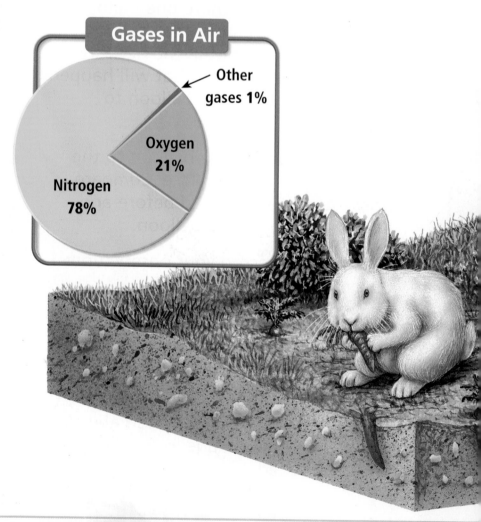

Gases in Air

Other gases 1%

Oxygen 21%

Nitrogen 78%

Living things depend on the gases in air to survive.

Nitrogen and oxygen are not the only gases that make up air. Small amounts of other substances are found in air. Two of these substances are carbon dioxide (KAHR-buhn dy-AHK syd) and water.

Carbon dioxide is a colorless, odorless gas that helps hold heat close to Earth. When you breathe out, you give off carbon dioxide. All animals give off carbon dioxide when they breathe. Plants use carbon dioxide to make food. In the process of making food, plants give off oxygen.

▶ **TEXT STRUCTURE** What are the two main gases in air? What helped you find the answer?

Plants use carbon dioxide in air to make food. When plants make food, they release oxygen into the air.

Animals use oxygen to get energy from food. Animals give off carbon dioxide.

Plants absorb nitrogen through their roots. Plants need nitrogen to grow.

Earth's Blanket

On a cold night, it is good to have a blanket to wrap around you. Earth has a blanket, too. Earth's blanket is a layer of gases called the **atmosphere** (AT muh sfihr). The Sun heats Earth, and the atmosphere holds the heat close to Earth's surface. This keeps Earth's surface at a comfortable temperature. The atmosphere also helps protect living things from harmful rays given off by the Sun.

Like all matter, air takes up space. When you blow into a balloon, the balloon gets bigger. That is because the air you put inside it takes up space. Air also has weight. The weight of air presses down on Earth's surface all the time. The weight of air as it presses down is called **air pressure** (PREHSH uhr). Your body is used to air pressure, so you do not feel it.

Suppose you travel to the top of a very high mountain. Compared with air at the base of the mountain, there are fewer particles of air and they are more spread out at the top of a mountain. So there is less air pressing down. This means air pressure on the mountain top is lower than air pressure at the base. Because the air particles are more spread out, people sometimes say that the air is thinner.

The atmosphere has four layers. The lowest layer is called the troposphere (TROHP uh sfihr). This layer begins at Earth's surface.

As the air becomes thinner, climbers of very high mountains cannot get enough oxygen with each breath. Climbers have to breathe oxygen from a supply that they carry.

Earth's weather occurs in the troposhere. **Weather** is the conditions of the atmosphere at a certain place and time.

The layer of the atmosphere above the troposphere is the stratosphere (STRAT uh sfihr). If you have ever flown in a jet plane, you may have been in the stratosphere. Above the weather the air is calm and the airplane ride is smoother. This layer keeps a lot of the harmful part of the Sun's rays from reaching Earth.

The mesosphere (MEHZ uh sfihr) is the next layer. Most meteors burn up when they reach this layer.

The top layer of the atmosphere is called the thermosphere (THUHRM uh sfihr). Space shuttles travel in Earth's thermosphere.

▶ **TEXT STRUCTURE** Use the labeled drawing to identify four layers of Earth's atmosphere.

Thermosphere

The thermosphere is from 80 km (50 mi) to 700 km (430 mi). Space begins at the top of this layer.

Mesosphere

The mesosphere reaches from 50 km (30 mi) to 80 km (50 mi) above Earth. The coldest temperatures in the atmosphere are found here.

Stratosphere

The stratosphere reaches 10 km (6 mi) to 50 km (30 mi) above Earth. The Sun's powerful rays heat up the stratosphere.

Troposphere

The troposphere begins at the ground and rises to 10 km (6 mi). The temperature decreases as the height increases.

Greenhouse Effect

If you have ever been in a greenhouse, you know it is warm inside. The air in a greenhouse is usually warmer than the air outside. The glass walls and roof of a greenhouse let in light and heat from the Sun. The glass traps the heat, letting little out. This keeps the plants inside warm.

The atmosphere keeps Earth warm in the same way. Earth's atmosphere lets in light and heat from the Sun. Some of the heat escapes into space, but most of the heat is held in by the atmosphere.

This natural heating of Earth is called the greenhouse effect. The **greenhouse effect** is the process by which heat from the Sun builds up near Earth's surface and is trapped there by the atmosphere. In recent years, carbon dioxide, methane, and other gases have begun to build up in the atmosphere. Some scientists warn that the increase of these gases will cause Earth's air to become warmer. This process is called global warming.

▶ **TEXT STRUCTURE** Use the diagram to explain the greenhouse effect.

How does a greenhouse keep plants warm on cold days?

The Greenhouse Effect

Sun

Gases in the atmosphere trap some of this heat and keep it close to Earth's surface.

Heat from the Sun passes through the atmosphere and is reflected from the surface of Earth.

Atmosphere

Visual Summary

Air is made of nitrogen, oxygen, and other gases. Living things need air to survive.

The atmosphere is a blanket of air that surrounds Earth. The air is thinner higher in the atmosphere.

The atmosphere acts as a natural greenhouse that keeps Earth warm.

 **for Home and School**

WRITING **Persuasive** Many scientists believe that carbon dioxide is building up in the atmosphere because so many cars burn gasoline. Write a letter to the editor of a newspaper to convince people to drive less. Suggest other ways to travel.

ART **Draw the Atmosphere** Make a large poster of the atmosphere, showing four layers. Draw birds, airplanes, meteors, mountain peaks, and other objects. Place each at the correct height. Label the heights of objects.

Review

❶ MAIN IDEA How does the atmosphere support life on Earth?

❷ VOCABULARY Write a sentence using the terms *atmosphere* and *weather*.

❸ READING SKILL: Text Structure Which section had the most information about the structure of the atmosphere?

❹ CRITICAL THINKING: Analyze Trees in forests absorb carbon dioxide and store it. When trees burn, carbon dioxide is released. Carbon dioxide increases the atmosphere's greenhouse effect. What would be the long-term effect on the atmosphere if large areas of forest were burned?

❺ INQUIRY SKILL: Compare How are the troposphere and the thermosphere different?

✔ TEST PREP The weight of air pressing down on an object is called ___.

A. the atmosphere.

B. weather.

C. oxygen.

D. air pressure.

Technology Visit **www.eduplace.com/scp/** to find out more about Earth's atmosphere.

D11

How Does the Water Cycle Affect Weather?

Why It Matters...

Animals have their own protection against bad weather. Birds' feathers offer some protection against the rain. But if it rains hard enough, birds will likely seek shelter, just as you would. You may not enjoy a rainy day, but rain is a necessary part of Earth's water cycle.

PREPARE TO INVESTIGATE

Inquiry Skill

Use Models You can use a model of an object, process, or idea to better understand or describe how it works.

Materials

- clear plastic container with lid
- water
- small resealable plastic bag
- 4–5 ice cubes
- lamp
- clock or watch
- metric ruler

Science and Math Toolbox

For step 1, review **Measuring Elapsed Time** on pages H12–H13.

Water Cycle Model

Procedure

1 **Collaborate** Work with a partner. In your *Science Notebook*, make a chart like the one shown.

2 **Measure** Use a metric ruler to measure 1 cm of water in a plastic container. Place the lid on the container.

3 Place 4 or 5 ice cubes in a plastic bag. Seal the bag and place it on the lid of the container.

4 **Use Models** Put the container near a lamp so that the lamp shines on one side of the container. **Safety:** Do not touch the light bulb. It may be very hot. Do not look directly into the light.

5 **Observe** After 15 minutes, carefully observe the container. Look for any changes on the inside and the outside of the container. Record your observations in your chart. Make observations every 15 minutes for one hour.

Conclusion

1. **Analyze Data** What changes occurred on the inside of the container?

2. **Use Models** You made a model of Earth's water cycle using a lamp as a source of heat. What source of heat warms the water in lakes, rivers, and oceans on Earth?

STEP 1

	Observations	
Time	Inside of Container	Outside of Container
Start		
After 15 minutes		
After 30 minutes		
After 45 minutes		
After 1 hour		

STEP 3

STEP 4

Investigate More!

Design an Experiment
Repeat the experiment, but put food coloring in the water. Compare what you see with what you saw in the first experiment. Write a hypothesis to explain the difference.

VOCABULARY

condensation	p. D15
evaporation	p. D15
precipitation	p. D16
water cycle	p. D16

READING SKILL

Sequence Use the chart to show events in the water cycle.

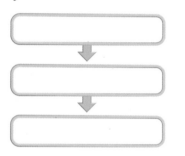

The Water Cycle and Weather

MAIN IDEA Water exists in three forms on Earth: as liquid water, as solid ice, and as a gas called water vapor. Water changes from one form to another in a process known as the water cycle.

Three States of Water

About three-fourths of Earth's surface is covered by water. Water is found on Earth in three forms, or states. Liquid water can be seen in oceans, seas, rivers, and rain. Ice is water in its solid state. Ice forms when heat is removed from liquid water. When temperatures fall below 0°C (32°F), liquid water freezes and becomes ice.

Water can also take the form of a gas. Water in gas form is called water vapor (VAY pur). Water vapor is in the air, but you cannot see it. It forms when heat is added to liquid water.

The lake in this photograph is partially frozen. What states of water can you see?

ice

You know that ice cubes will melt if they are warmed up. When heat is added to ice, the ice melts and changes to liquid water. Heat from the Sun melts the ice on the lake shown here. If more heat is added, the water gets warmer. Heat can also change liquid water to water vapor. This change is called evaporation (ih VAP uh ray shuhn). **Evaporation** is the change of state from liquid to gas. Even on a cold day, heat from the Sun can make some water from the lake evaporate.

The mist that you can see above the surface of the lake is not water vapor. It is a cloud of tiny drops of water in the air. The drops of water formed by condensation (kahn-dehn SAY shuhn). **Condensation** is the change of state from gas to liquid. Water vapor in the air came from lake water that evaporated. When the air above the lake cooled, the water vapor in the air condensed. It changed form and became a liquid again. The drops of condensed water are so small that they stay in the air and form a cloud of mist that you can see.

▶ **SEQUENCE** Identify, in order, each change in state when water evaporates and then condenses.

water vapor

liquid water

The Water Cycle

The water on Earth changes from one form to another over and over again as it goes through the water cycle (SY kuhl). The **water cycle** is the movement of water into the air as water vapor and back to Earth's surface as precipitation (prih sihp-uh TAY shuhn). **Precipitation** is any form of water that falls from clouds to Earth's surface.

Water in oceans, lakes, and rivers evaporates and becomes water vapor. As water vapor rises in the air, it cools and condenses into water droplets. These droplets form clouds.

As more water vapor condenses, the drops become heavier and form drops which fall to Earth as precipitation.

Some precipitation flows downhill on Earth's surface as runoff. Runoff water flows toward streams, rivers, lakes, and oceans. Some precipitation flows down into the ground to become groundwater.

The water cycle cleans Earth's water supply. For example, salt and other materials in the ocean are left behind when ocean water evaporates.

Water Cycle Water moves into the air as a gas and back to Earth's surface as a liquid in the water cycle.

precipitation
Water droplets in the cloud become heavy, and they fall as precipitation.

evaporation
Heat from the Sun causes evaporation of water from oceans, lakes, and rivers. Water vapor rises in the air and cools.

Types of Clouds

Clouds form when water vapor in the air condenses. A cloud that forms close to the ground is called fog.

Stratus (STRAT uhs) clouds are low-level clouds that form in layers. Stratus clouds usually bring steady rain.

Cumulus (KYOOM yoo luhs) clouds are fluffy and have flat bases. They form low in the sky. They usually mean fair weather.

Cirrus (SEER uhs) clouds are thin, feathery clouds made of ice crystals. They form high in the sky. Cirrus clouds indicate fair weather.

Cumulonimbus (kyoom yoo lo NIHM buhs) clouds bring thunderstorms.

▶ **SEQUENCE** What causes clouds to form? What step in the water cycle comes before this process?

Stratus

Cumulus

Cirrus

Cumulonimbus

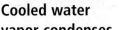
condensation
Cooled water vapor condenses into water droplets and forms clouds.

Rain consists of falling drops of liquid water.

Sleet forms when rain freezes as it falls.

Snowflakes can form in many different shapes.

A hailstone can be as large as a baseball.

Forms of Precipitation

Precipitation is any form of water that falls from clouds to Earth. Rain, snow, sleet, and hail are all forms of precipitation.

Rain is the most common form of precipitation. It rains when drops of water in clouds fall through air that is above freezing.

Sleet is rain that freezes as it falls. If the temperature near Earth's surface is below freezing, rain turns to ice before it strikes the ground.

Snow falls when the temperature in a cloud is below freezing. Water vapor in the cloud forms ice crystals known as snowflakes.

Hail forms when drops of rain freeze and strong winds carry them higher into a cloud. As hailstones fall again, more ice forms on them. They become larger. This process can happen over and over. Finally, when the hailstones are too heavy to be lifted by the wind, they fall.

▶ **SEQUENCE** Describe the repeating process that forms hail.

Visual Summary

Water exists in three states: solid ice, liquid water, and water vapor.

The water cycle is the movement of water into the air as water vapor and back to Earth as precipitation.

There are different types of clouds and precipitation.

LINKS for Home and School

MATH Calculate Water Use Every time you shower, wash your hands, or water a plant, you are using water. Each person in the United States uses about 277 liters of water every day. Find out how much water each person uses in one week. How much water does each person use in one year?

SOCIAL STUDIES Find Record-Breaking Hail Use the Internet to find out where the largest hailstone on record fell. Share what you learned with the class.

Review

1 MAIN IDEA Describe the stages of the water cycle.

2 VOCABULARY What does the term *precipitation* mean?

3 READING SKILL: Sequence During a storm, rain falls to Earth's surface. The water runs into a river and out into the ocean. What happens to the water next?

4 CRITICAL THINKING: Evaluate Suppose someone tells you that snowflakes are frozen raindrops. Is this statement true? Explain.

5 INQUIRY SKILL: Use Models Suppose you leave a cup of water on the windowsill and the water disappears. What part of the water cycle did you model?

TEST PREP Tall clouds that produce thunderstorms are called ___.

A. cirrus.

B. cumulonimbus.

C. stratus.

D. cumulus.

Technology Visit www.eduplace.com/scp/ to learn more about the water cycle.

What Causes Weather?

Why It Matters...

Mt. Washington in New Hampshire is nicknamed "Home of the World's Worst Weather." Scientists here record weather conditions and conduct important research. The research includes testing instruments that can help scientists accurately predict the weather.

PREPARE TO INVESTIGATE

Inquiry Skill

Analyze Data When you analyze data, you look for patterns that can help you make predictions, hypotheses, and generalizations.

Materials

- barometer
- thermometer
- precipitation gauge
- local newspaper weather map and weather forecast

Science and Math Toolbox

For step 5, review **Using a Thermometer** on page H8.

Local Forecast

Procedure

1. **Collaborate** Work in groups of 3 or 4. In your *Science Notebook*, make a chart like the one shown.

2. **Measure** Set a barometer outside. Read it immediately and then again after one hour. Note whether the air pressure is rising, falling, or unchanged.

3. **Research** Look on the Internet and in reference books to learn about barometer readings. Find out what type of weather usually follows a rising or falling barometer reading. Predict the day's weather based on your barometer readings. Record your prediction.

4. **Analyze Data** Study a newspaper weather map and forecast. In your chart, record the newspaper's forecast.

5. **Measure** Set a thermometer and precipitation gauge outside in an open area. Check and record the temperature and the depth of any rain or snow that falls throughout the day. Also, record the cloud cover and wind conditions.

Conclusion

1. **Compare** How did your weather prediction compare to the newspaper's weather forecast?

2. **Analyze Data** Did the actual weather match the newspaper's forecast? Did it match your prediction? Explain.

STEP 1

	My Weather Prediction	Newspaper Weather Forecast	Actual Weather
Temperature			
Precipitation			
Wind			
Clouds			

STEP 2

STEP 5

Investigate More!

Research Use the Internet, the library, and local sources to find out how weather scientists make your local weather forecast. Write a report about the instruments and tools they use.

Learn by Reading

▶ **VOCABULARY**

air mass	p. D25
front	p. D26

▶ **READING SKILL**

Main Idea and Details As you read, write down the main idea and two details.

A hurricane is severe weather. High winds, lots of rain, high humidity, and low air pressure are usual conditions for this type of storm.

Weather

MAIN IDEA Scientist gather data about temperature, humidity, wind, and air pressure. They use this information to make predictions about weather.

Weather Factors

On a fair day, you might describe the weather with one just word, such as "sunny" or "warm." Scientists talk about many more factors when they describe the weather. Weather involves all of the conditions of the atmosphere at a certain time and place. They include temperature, amount of water vapor in the air, wind, and air pressure.

The temperature is how hot or cold the air is. The amount of water vapor in the air is called humidity (hyoo MIHD uh tee). High humidity can make the air feel wet and sticky. Wind is the movement of air. Recall that air pressure is the weight of air as it presses down on Earth's surface.

Each weather factor can be measured using a different instrument. A thermometer measures the temperature of the air. A rain gauge collects and measures precipitation. An anemometer (an uh MAHM uh tuhr) is a tool used to measure the speed of the wind. Air pressure is measured with a device called a barometer (buh RAH muh tur). It tells whether air pressure is high or low.

▶ **MAIN IDEA** What are the main weather factors?

Thermometer
A thermometer measures temperature in degrees Celsius or degrees Fahrenheit.

Rain Gauge
A rain gauge measures the amount of precipitation that has fallen in an area.

Barometer A barometer measures air pressure in units called millibars.

Anemometer
The cups on the anemometer spin in the wind. The anemometer calculates the wind speed in kilometers an hour or miles an hour.

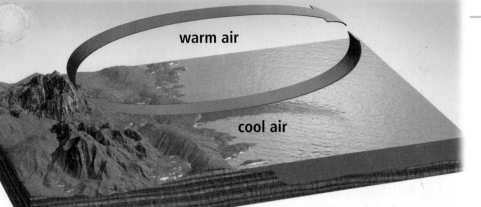

During the day, cool ocean breezes move toward the land.

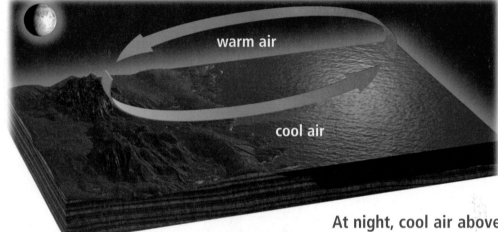

At night, cool air above the land moves toward the ocean.

Wind

You probably know that wind is moving air. But what makes air move? Air flows from areas of high pressure to areas of low pressure. High-pressure areas and low-pressure areas result from the way Earth's surface is heated by the Sun.

During the day, surfaces on Earth absorb, or take in, heat from the Sun. Land areas become warm very quickly. The land warms the air above it. As the air warms, it expands. This expanding of air produces an area of low pressure. The warm, light air that is above the land begins to rise.

Oceans change temperature slowly, so they do not become as warm as the land. During the day, air above the ocean is not as warm as air over the land. As the warm air above the land begins to rise, the cooler, heavier air above the ocean moves in to take its place. This flow of cool air from the ocean to the land is known as a sea breeze.

At night, the land cools off more quickly than the ocean water does. In this case, the air above the ocean is warmer and lighter than the air above the land. As the warm air rises, the cool air above the land moves toward the ocean.

Air Masses

You have seen that land and water absorb different amounts of heat from the Sun. Areas near the equator (ee KWAY tur) receive more heat from sunlight than areas near the poles. The equator is an imaginary line around Earth and is an equal distance from the North Pole and the South Pole.

Each area warms or cools the air above it, creating an air mass. An **air mass** is a large body of air that has about the same temperature, air pressure, and moisture throughout.

Air masses are described by two conditions—temperature and humidity. They are either warm or cold and they are either moist or dry. Air masses that form near the equator are usually warm. Air masses that form near the poles are cold. Air masses that form over the oceans are moist. Those that form over the land areas are usually dry. Most changes in weather occur when one air mass moves into an area and pushes out another air mass.

▶ **MAIN IDEA** What conditions describe air masses?

The arrows show the movement of air masses that affect the United States.

A polar land air mass brings cold, dry air to the northern Midwest during the winter.

A polar ocean air mass brings cool, moist air to the Pacific Northwest.

A polar ocean air mass in the Atlantic Ocean keeps the Northeast cool and wet.

A tropical ocean air mass brings wet winters to California and the Pacific coast.

A tropical land air mass brings extremely hot, dry air to the Southwest.

A tropical ocean air mass brings warm, wet weather from the Gulf of Mexico to the South.

Weather Patterns

Air masses do not stay over the areas where they form. As Earth rotates, air masses move. In North America, most air masses move from west to east. As the air masses move, they bump into each other. The place where two air masses meet is called a **front**. A front moves across Earth's surface as one air mass pushes against the other. The weather can change very suddenly when a front moves across an area. Most storms and precipitation take place along fronts.

A cold front forms as a cold air mass meets a warm air mass. The cold air moves under the warm air, pushing it up. As the warm air rises, clouds form and precipitation occurs. Thunderstorms often happen along a cold front.

A warm front forms as a warm air mass pushes into a cold air mass. The warm air slowly moves up over the cold air. Layers of gray clouds and steady precipitation are seen when a warm front moves into an area.

The same types of air masses usually form over North America each year. The air masses usually move in the same direction each year. This creates weather patterns that repeat with the seasons. For example, a cold air mass moves down from Canada. A warm air mass moves up from the Gulf of Mexico. Every spring and summer these air masses collide over the Great Plains. The cold front causes the violent thunderstorms and tornadoes that give the area the nickname Tornado Alley.

Analyzing Weather Data

A meteorologist (mee tee uh-RAHL uh jihst) is a scientist who studies weather. Studying weather involves measuring conditions near Earth's surface and high in the atmosphere. Scientists gather weather data from observatories, weather balloons, airplanes, and satellites in space.

Meteorologists use the data they collect to identify the kinds of air masses over an area. They also predict what kind of front will form and where that front will move. This type of information is used to produce a weather map. Weather maps are often printed in newspapers as part of a weather forecast. A forecast is a prediction of what the weather will be for a particular day, week, or longer period of time.

▶ MAIN IDEA Where does most precipitation occur?

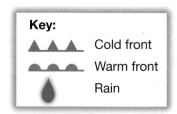

Key:

▲▲▲ Cold front

⬤⬤⬤ Warm front

🌢 Rain

▲ Weather maps use symbols to show the location of fronts and precipitation.

◀ A cold front can cause a line of powerful thunderstorms that moves from west to east across the United States.

Severe Weather

Weather forecasts can help you decide if you should wear a jacket to school. But weather forecasts can also help save lives. Earth's weather can be deadly. Severe weather includes hurricanes, tornadoes, and snowstorms. Hurricanes often produce floods and strong winds. Severe storms, including hurricanes and blizzards, can destroy property and put people in harm's way.

Meterologists study storms using satellites in space and weather instruments on the ground. Forecasters issue weather warnings when severe weather is likely to move into an area. These warnings can save lives by giving people time to prepare for a storm. Warnings can also allow people to leave an area that is in the path of dangerous weather.

▶ **MAIN IDEA** Identify three kinds of severe weather.

A hurricane is a huge swirling storm that forms over the ocean. Note that winds flow counter clockwise. ▼

Land and Water

Procedure

1. **Collaborate** Work with a partner. Sprinkle a large amount of salt on a sheet of black construction paper. Use a rolling pin to grind the salt into the paper. The paper should be covered with white powder. **Safety:** Wear goggles.

STEP 1

2. **Use Models** Fold the black paper in half, with the salt-covered side facing out. Set the paper in an empty aquarium so it stands up in a tent shape to model a mountain.

STEP 2

3. **Use Models** Place a pan of hot water in the aquarium next to one side of the "mountain." Cover the aquarium with a sheet of cardboard.

4. **Observe** After 10 minutes, remove the cover. Observe each side of the mountain. Record your observations and draw a sketch in your *Science Notebook*.

STEP 3

Conclusion

1. **Analyze Data** What happened to the salt on each side of the mountain?

2. **Hypothesize** What might have caused the change in the way the salt appeared?

3. **Use Models** If the paper models a mountain, what might the pan of water stand for? Use your observations to describe what the weather conditions might be like in an area similar to your model.

Investigate More!

Research Use an atlas or other maps to find places on Earth where the surface features look like your model. Use the Internet and the library to find out what kinds of weather conditions exist in these areas.

Climates of the World

VOCABULARY

climate   p. D34
polar climate   p. D35
temperate
  climate   p. D35
tropical climate p. D35

READING SKILL

Cause and Effect As you read, write down the causes of changes in climate.

MAIN IDEA Climate refers to the average long-term weather conditions. Climate changes with latitude, altitude, and over time.

Major Climate Zones

If someone asked you what winter is like in your area, what would you say? You could not say exactly what the temperature would be or how much snow or rain would fall on a certain day. But you probably could give someone a general idea of the weather in your area during the winter. You would be describing your climate (KLY muht). **Climate** is the average weather conditions in an area over a long period of time. The climate of an area determines the kinds of plants and animals that can live there.

Colorful tropical fish can only survive in hot climates where the water temperature is warm.

Skunks are hardy animals that can survive both warm summers and cold winters.

Harp seals live in cold climates. Their thick fur keeps them warm.

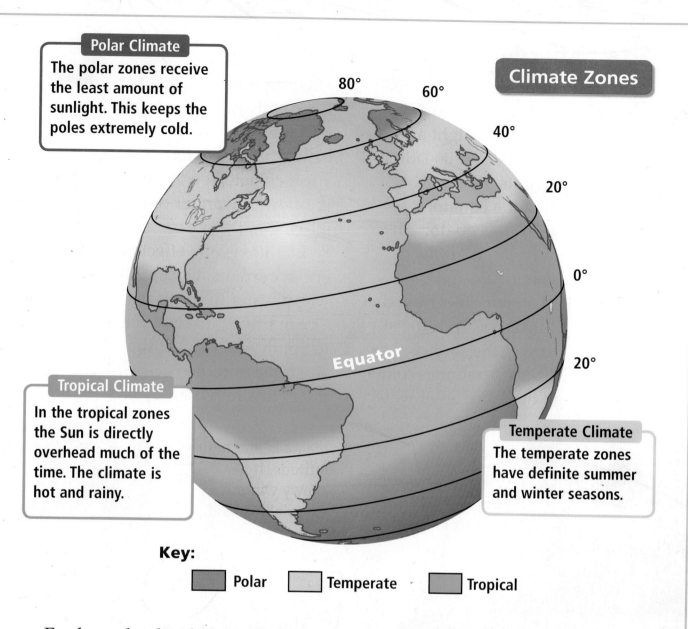

Polar Climate
The polar zones receive the least amount of sunlight. This keeps the poles extremely cold.

80° 60° 40° 20° 0° 20°

Equator

Tropical Climate
In the tropical zones the Sun is directly overhead much of the time. The climate is hot and rainy.

Temperate Climate
The temperate zones have definite summer and winter seasons.

Key:

☐ Polar ☐ Temperate ☐ Tropical

Earth can be divided into three major climate zones. The warmest climates are found in the tropical climate zone. A **tropical climate** is hot and rainy. The tropical climate zone is the area directly north and south of the equator. It receives strong sunlight all year.

The coldest climate zones are the areas around the North Pole and the South Pole. The poles receive the least amount of sunlight on Earth. Because of this, a **polar climate** has very cold temperatures all through the year. Most places in the polar climate zones have snow on the ground almost all year.

Most of the United States is in a temperate (TEHM pur iht) zone. The temperate zones are between the tropical zone and the polar zones. A **temperate climate** usually has warm, dry summers and cold, wet winters.

▶ **CAUSE AND EFFECT** What causes a polar climate to be so cold?

D35

Factors Affecting Climate

The amount of sunlight an area receives has a large effect on its climate. How much sunlight an area receives depends on its latitude (LAT ih-tood), or its distance north or south of the equator. Low latitudes are near the equator. The Sun is high in the sky and the temperature is hot.

High latitudes are farther from the equator. The Sun is lower in the sky and sunlight strikes the surface at an angle. The temperature is colder.

Oceans and other bodies of water also affect the climate of an area. A large body of water usually causes the climate of nearby land areas to be wet and mild. Ocean currents affect climate, too. An ocean current is a flow of warmer or colder water moving in the ocean.

El Niño is one effect of changing ocean currents. During El Niño, warm water in the eastern Pacific Ocean brings more rain than usual to South America. At the same time, Australia and the Pacific Islands get much less rain than usual.

Oregon

Oregon is at a high latitude. But ocean currents warm the coast.

Maine is at a high latitude. It has cold, snowy winters, especially inland.

Maine

45°

40°

35°

30°

25°

Florida

Florida is at a low latitude. Its climate is warm.

Altitude (AL tih tood), or height above sea level, also affects climate. The higher you travel up a mountain, the colder it gets.

The Alps are a group of high mountains in Europe. Most of Europe has a mild temperate climate. But the altitude at the top of the Alps is great enough to keep temperatures cold. For this reason, there is a covering of snow on some of these mountaintops all year round.

Mountains can affect climate in other ways. Mountains can block the path of air masses. When a warm, wet air mass reaches a mountain, the air mass is forced upward. The air mass cools as it rises. The water vapor in the air mass condenses and falls on the mountain as precipitation.

When the air mass moves over the mountain, the air is dry. The land on the other side of the mountain might get so little precipitation that it is a desert.

▶ **CAUSE AND EFFECT** **What are three factors that affect climate?**

The tops of the Alps are cold and snowy. The climate at the base of the Alps is fairly mild. Different plants and animals live at different altitudes.

How Climates Have Changed

The climate in the area where you live has probably been the same for many years. But climates do not stay the same forever. They can change both in specific areas and over the whole Earth.

Much of North America was covered by ice about 20,000 years ago. Woolly mammoths and saber-toothed tigers roamed the Great Plains. Since this period, known as an ice age, Earth's climate has become warmer. Many scientists believe that Earth's climate may still be warming.

Scientists find information about climate in unusual ways. They look at tree rings in ancient fossils to learn what the climate was like when the tree was alive. Scientists have also taken core samples of ice from Antarctica, at the South Pole. This ice can be hundreds of thousands of years old. Each layer contains traces of air from long ago. These ice core samples have helped scientists understand how climates have changed.

▶ **CAUSE AND EFFECT** What has damaged a protective layer of Earth's atmosphere?

A protective layer of Earth's atmosphere has been damaged by certain chemicals. The damaged part, shown in purple, allows harmful rays from the Sun to reach Earth's surface. ▼

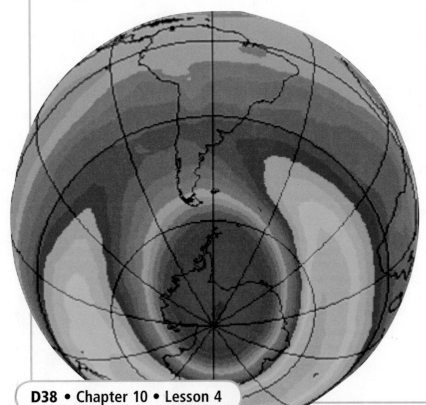

▲ Each layer of an ice core contains bits of dust, gases, and other materials. Scientists can tell what the atmosphere was like in the past by studying ice cores.

Lesson Wrap-Up

Visual Summary

Climate is the average weather conditions of an area over many years.

There are three major climate zones on Earth: tropical, temperate, and polar.

Latitude, altitude, and bodies of water can affect the climate of an area. Climates change over time.

LINKS for Home and School

MATH **Calculating Mass** The mass of one woolly mammoth is 5,700 kg. Another mammoth has a mass of 6,900 kg. What is the difference in the mass of the mammoths?

TECHNOLOGY **Research on Coping With Climate** Humans use technology to help them survive in different climates. As a class, brainstorm a list of the technologies that help people survive and be comfortable in various climates. Work in groups to research one technology and give a short presentation about it to the class.

Review

❶ MAIN IDEA What are two factors that affect climate?

❷ VOCABULARY Write a sentence about a tropical climate.

❸ READING SKILL: Cause and Effect What climate factor allows people in mountain areas to ski during summer months?

❹ CRITICAL THINKING: Synthesize Kilimanjaro is a tall mountain in Africa close to the equator. What do you think the climate is like at the base of Kilimanjaro? What would the climate be like at the top?

❺ INQUIRY SKILL: Use Models Suppose you place a lamp on a table next to a globe. Which part of the globe will warm up the most?

✔ TEST PREP

Denver, Colorado, is at a higher altitude than Abilene, Kansas. The climate in Denver is probably ___ than the climate in Abilene.

A. wetter

B. drier

C. hotter

D. colder

Technology
Visit **www.eduplace.com/scp/** to find out more about the causes of weather.

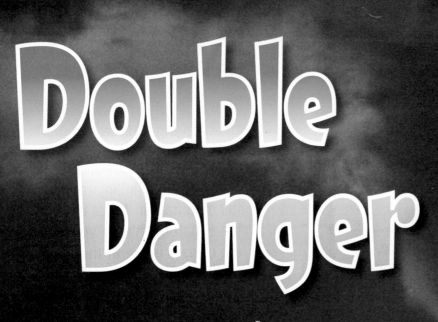

Double Danger

Better take cover! Here come two of nature's most powerful forces—tornadoes and lightning! Both are formed by the extreme energy of thunderstorms.

A tornado is a violent, twisting funnel of wind that stretches from a thunderstorm to the ground. Lightning is a powerful discharge of electricity caused by a build up of electrical charges. Both can be extremely destructive.

There is much that scientists still don't understand about how tornadoes and lightning form. Even so, weather scientists have been able to save many lives by storm alerts and by showing people how to protect themselves from these powerhouses of weather.

Extreme Wind

Tornadoes can produce wind speeds up to 300 miles per hour, causing incredible damage.

Extreme Electricity

If it were controlled, one lightning bolt could power 10 million homes for a full month. Instead, all that energy is released in a flash.

Vocabulary

Complete each sentence with a term from the list.

1. The process in which liquid changes to gas is called _____.

2. A place that has very cold temperatures year round has a/an _____.

3. The place where two air masses meet is a/an _____.

4. The trapping of heat by Earth's atmosphere is called the _____.

5. A large body of air that has about the same temperature, air pressure, and moisture throughout is a/an _____.

6. Any form of water that falls from clouds is called _____.

7. An area with warm, dry summers and cold, wet winters has a/an _____.

8. The change of state from gas to liquid is called _____.

9. The blanket of air that surrounds Earth is the _____.

10. The weight of air as it pushes down on Earth's surface is called _____.

air mass D25
air pressure D8
atmosphere D8
climate D34
condensation D15
evaporation D15
front D26
greenhouse effect D10
polar climate D35
precipitation D16
temperate climate D35
tropical climate D35
water cycle D16
weather D9

Test Prep

Write the letter of the best answer choice.

11. A tropical climate is _____.

   A. hot and dry.
   B. hot and rainy.
   C. cold and dry.
   D. cold and rainy.

12. The movement of water into the atmosphere as water vapor and back to Earth's surface as precipitation is known as _____.

   A. climate.
   B. temperate zone.
   C. air pressure.
   D. the water cycle.

13. The conditions of the atmosphere at a certain place and time is called _____.

   A. air
   B. weather
   C. climate
   D. season

14. The average weather conditions in an area over a long period of time is _____.

   A. climate.
   B. weather.
   C. greenhouse effect.
   D. forecast.

15. **Compare** Compare and contrast a warm front and a cold front. What type of weather does each bring to an area?

16. **Use Models** You have three types of materials: puffy cotton balls; thick, layered gray blankets; and thin, wispy fibers. Which type of cloud could you model with each material?

Map the Concept

Label the diagram with the terms listed below.

wind
air pressure
temperature

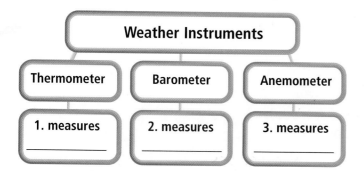

Weather Instruments

Thermometer	Barometer	Anemometer
1. measures _____	2. measures _____	3. measures _____

17. **Evaluate** A certain kind of plant requires a great deal of water and sunlight. In which climate would it grow best, a polar climate, a tropical climate, or a temperate climate?

18. **Analyze** Use what you know about altitude to explain why a mountain may have snow at the top but not at the bottom.

19. **Apply** How would you describe the climate in your area? How might the latitude, land forms, bodies of water, and air masses of your area affect your climate?

20. **Synthesize** Plants and animals rely on each other for gases each needs to breathe. Explain why this is so.

Performance Assessment

Make a Weather Map
Use a blank map of your state to create a weather map. Choose a recent day. Use the Internet, newspapers, and library resources to find out the kinds of weather that existed throughout the state on that day. Use weather map symbols to show what the weather was like.

Chapter 11

Looking at the Universe

LESSON 1

From the center of the solar system, the Sun's energy reaches Earth—how does this energy support life on the planet?

Read about it in Lesson 1.

LESSON 2

From the rings of Saturn and Uranus to the many moons of Jupiter—what is known about the outer planets of the solar system?

Read about it in Lesson 2.

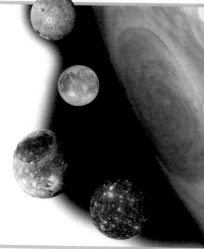

LESSON 3

Seasons turn and day becomes night— what causes these changes?

Read about it in Lesson 3.

LESSON 4

From glowing balls of hot gas to tiny dots of light that spill across the night sky—what are stars and galaxies?

Read about it in Lesson 4.

How Is the Sun Important to Earth?

Why It Matters...

Without the Sun, Earth would be a lifeless, frozen rock. Light and heat from the Sun allow life to exist on Earth. The Sun warms the land, the oceans, and the atmosphere. Plants could not grow without energy from the Sun. In fact, the Sun is the source of almost all energy on Earth.

PREPARE TO INVESTIGATE

Inquiry Skill

Collaborate When you collaborate, you work as a team to collect data, listen to others, and share your ideas.

Materials

- 3 shallow bowls
- sand
- soil
- water
- 3 thermometers
- lamp with 100-watt bulb
- clock or watch
- goggles

Science and Math Toolbox

For step 5, review **Using a Thermometer** on page H8.

Sun Effects
Procedure

STEP 1

Model of Sun and Earth	Starting Temperature	Final Temperature
Sand		
Soil		
Water		

1. **Collaborate** Work in a small group. In your *Science Notebook*, make a chart like the one shown.

2. Half fill a bowl with sand. Half fill a second bowl with soil. Half fill a third bowl with water. **Safety**: Wear goggles.

3. **Measure** Place a thermometer in each bowl. The bulb of each thermometer should be covered the same amount. Wait 2 minutes. Then check and record the temperature in each bowl.

STEP 2

4. **Predict** Place the three bowls close together under a lamp. The light should hit all three bowls equally. Predict how the temperature of each material will change after 30 minutes. **Safety:** Do not touch the light bulb. It may be very hot.

STEP 4

5. **Measure** After 30 minutes, read the thermometers. Record in your chart the temperature of each material.

Conclusion

1. **Compare** Which material is warmest after 30 minutes? How did your results compare with your predictions?

2. **Infer** Would a light-colored or a dark-colored material heat faster in sunlight?

3. **Use Models** What can you infer from your model about how the Sun affects sand, water, and soil on Earth?

Investigate More!

Be an Inventor Design a doghouse that is heated by sunlight. Choose materials for the doghouse that heat up quickly in sunlight. Describe how you would build it and where it should be placed.

VOCABULARY

gravity	p. D52
orbit	p. D50
planet	p. D50
solar system	p. D50

READING SKILL

Draw Conclusions Use facts from the lesson to draw a conclusion about the Sun's effect on Earth.

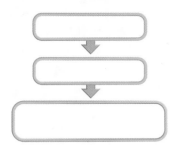

Earth's Star

MAIN IDEA The Sun provides the energy that supports life on Earth.

Energy from the Sun

If you stand outside on a sunny day, you can feel the warmth of sunlight on your skin. Energy from the Sun warms you. It also warms Earth's land and water.

Land and water heat up at different rates. Water warms more slowly than sand and soil do. This means that oceans, lakes, and other bodies of water warm more slowly than the land near them. Bodies of water also cool more slowly than the land near them.

The uneven heating of Earth causes wind. Earth's surface is heated and warms the air above it. Some areas of Earth are heated more than others. So the air above these areas is warmed more. The warmer air rises. Cooler air moves in to take its place. This movement of air is wind.

The Sun's diameter is 109 times the diameter of Earth. In this picture, they are shown much closer together than they really are.

Sun

Earth

Energy from the Sun heats Earth's water. Water heats up slowly, but it also cools more slowly than land.

Plants use the Sun's energy to make food. Animals get this energy by eating plants or animals that eat plants.

Some areas of Earth's surface are heated by the Sun's energy more than others. The uneven heating causes wind.

The Sun's energy powers the water cycle. It causes water on Earth to evaporate, forming water vapor.

Energy from the Sun keeps water moving through the water cycle. When the Sun heats water on Earth's surface, some of the water evaporates. It enters the air as water vapor. Clouds form when water vapor in air cools and condenses into tiny drops. When the drops of water are large enough, they fall to Earth as rain.

The Sun provides plants with energy to make food. Green plants use the energy in sunlight to make food in the process of photosynthesis (foh toh SIHN-thih sihs). In this way a plant stores the Sun's energy. When an animal eats the plant, some of that stored energy is passed on to the animal. Other animals eat the plant-eating animals, so they get energy from the Sun, too.

▶ **DRAW CONCLUSIONS** **How does an animal get energy from the Sun?**

The Sun and Solar System

You know that the Sun is a star. Like all stars, the Sun makes its own light. Earth and the Moon do not make their own light. Moonlight is really light from the Sun that bounces off the Moon's surface.

Earth is a **planet**, or large body made of rock or gas that moves around a star. Earth's path as it travels around the Sun is called its **orbit** (AWR biht). A moon is a body that moves in an orbit around a planet.

The Sun is at the center of the solar system (SOH lur SIHS tuhm). The **solar system** is made up of the Sun, eight planets, and other smaller bodies that orbit the Sun. There are many moons in the solar system, including Earth's Moon.

▶ **DRAW CONCLUSIONS** When astronauts on the Moon looked at Earth, why did it look bright?

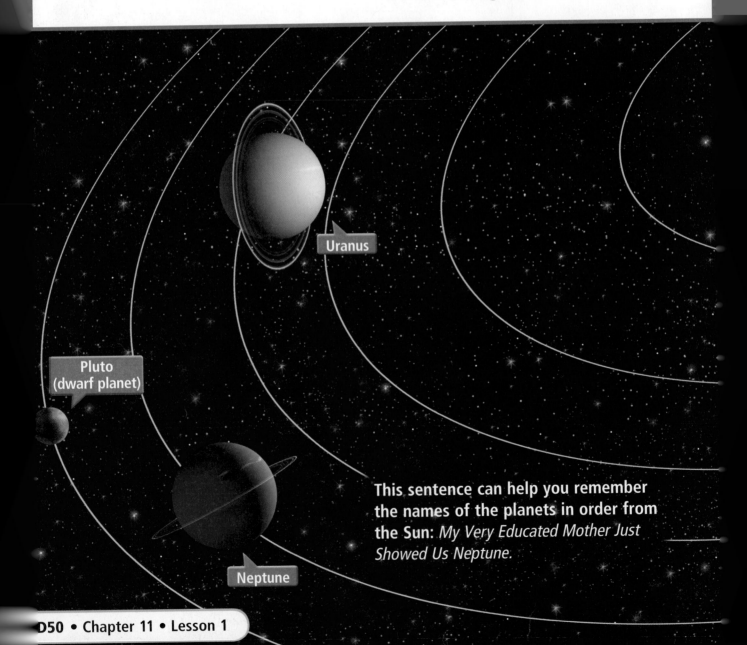

Uranus

Pluto (dwarf planet)

Neptune

This sentence can help you remember the names of the planets in order from the Sun: *My Very Educated Mother Just Showed Us Neptune.*

Saturn

Mars

Moon

Earth

Sun

Mercury

Venus

Jupiter

Comparing the Sun, Earth, and Moon

Body	Diameter	Mass	Surface
Sun	1,393,000 km (864,950 mi)	333,000 times the mass of Earth	Very hot gases on the Sun's surface are always in motion.
Earth	12,756 km (7,918 mi)	About 6 trillion trillion kg	Earth's surface is covered mostly by water, rock, and soil.
Moon	3,475 km (2,160 mi)	About $\frac{1}{80}$ of the mass of Earth	The surface of the Moon is dry and dusty. It has mountains and craters but no atmosphere.

Gravity

You have probably heard someone say, "What goes up must come down." No matter how high you can jump, you come back to Earth. What pulls you back? The answer is gravity (GRAV ih tee). **Gravity** is the force that pulls bodies or objects toward other bodies or objects. When you jump, this force pulls you toward Earth. Gravity also keeps the planets orbiting the Sun.

The Sun, the planets, and the Moon all have gravity. They pull on each other. But they pull with different amounts of force. The amount of gravity that a body has depends on its mass, or how much matter it contains.

The mass of Earth is greater than the mass of the Moon. So Earth's gravity is stronger than the Moon's. You would weigh less on the Moon than you do on Earth. For example, someone who weighs 65 pounds on Earth weighs only 11 pounds on the Moon. You could also jump higher on the Moon than on Earth.

▶ **DRAW CONCLUSIONS** Earth's gravity pulls on you at the same time that your gravity pulls on Earth. Which pull is stronger?

A great deal of force is needed to overcome the pull of Earth's gravity and lift the rockets and space shuttle into space.

Visual Summary

Plants and animals use the Sun's energy to live. The Sun's energy causes wind and powers the water cycle.

The Sun is at the center of the solar system, which includes eight planets and their moons.

Gravity pulls objects toward Earth. The Sun's gravity keeps each planet in its orbit.

LINKS for Home and School

MATH **Calculate Leap Years** An Earth year is actually slightly longer than 365 days so we have "leap years" of 366 days. A leap year is any year divisible by 4, except for years that end 00. These years must be divisible by 400. Which of the following years were leap years? (a) 1900 (b) 1704 (c) 1800 (d) 1969 (e) 2000

SOCIAL STUDIES Write a Song
Research the Sun-worshipping practices of the Inca, the Egyptians, or the American Plains Indians. Make up a song about the Sun that one of these cultures might have performed.

Review

1 **MAIN IDEA** How does the Sun support life on Earth?

2 **VOCABULARY** What is the solar system?

3 **READING SKILL: Draw Conclusions** Why would an astronaut be able to lift heavy equipment more easily on the Moon than on Earth?

4 **CRITICAL THINKING: Analyze** What is one way the size of Earth and the size of the Moon can be compared?

5 **INQUIRY SKILL: Collaborate** Work with three other students to make a list of the Sun's effects on Earth. Explain one of the effects and give an example of how it affects your daily life.

TEST PREP
Gravity is the force that ___.

A. causes wind.

B. supports life on Earth.

C. makes things float in space.

D. keeps the planets in orbit around the Sun.

Technology
Visit **www.eduplace.com/scp/** to find out more about the Sun.

What Are the Outer Planets?

Why It Matters...

All through recorded history, people have made observations about the objects they saw in the sky. Since the 1600s they have used telescopes to make those observations. Now scientists can send spacecraft to other planets to get a closer look.

PREPARE TO INVESTIGATE

Inquiry Skill

Measure When you measure, you use tools to find the size, volume, mass, or temperature of an object.

Materials

- 2 large sheets of construction paper
- metric ruler
- pencil
- scissors

Science and Math Toolbox

For step 2, review **Using a Tape Measure or Ruler** on page H6.

Outer Planets

Procedure

STEP 1

Order in the Solar System	Smallest to Largest	Largest to Smallest

1. In your *Science Notebook*, make a chart like the one shown.

2. **Measure** For each measurement below, use a metric ruler to draw a line of that length on construction paper. Draw another line perpendicular to the first line. Connect the lines to make a circle. Label each circle with the name of the planet it represents.

   Jupiter   23 cm
   Saturn   19 cm
   Uranus   8.2 cm
   Neptune   7.6 cm

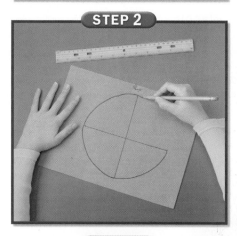

STEP 2

3. **Use a Model** Cut out and label each planet. Put the model planets in the order they are in the solar system, as listed. Record this data in your chart.

4. **Compare** Put your model planets in order from smallest to largest. Record the data. Put your model planets in order from largest to smallest. Record the data.

STEP 3

Conclusion

1. **Analyze Data** Compare your data. Which two sets of data are similar?

2. **Infer** Refer to the data about planet size on D57. What can you infer about the relationship between planet size and distance from the Sun?

Investigate More!

Research Use the Internet or library sources to find pictures and other information about the outer planets. Use the information to make planet data cards.

The Outer Planets

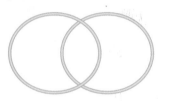

READING SKILL

Compare and Contrast
Use a Venn diagram to show similarities and differences between two planets.

MAIN IDEA The four planets farthest from the Sun are called the outer planets.

Earth's Neighbors

Earth and its neighbors, Mercury, Venus, and Mars, are the four planets closest to the Sun. They are called the inner planets. The inner planets are smaller than the other planets in the solar system. The inner planets all formed from dense rock. Although they are made of similar materials, they are not exactly alike. Earth has one moon revolving around it. Mars has two small moons. Neither Mercury nor Venus has a moon.

Mercury

Mercury has many large and small craters. These craters are very old. There are plains between the craters.

Venus

Venus has highlands and rolling hills as Earth's land areas do. Venus also has lowlands much like Earth's ocean floors.

Mars

Mars has a dusty, reddish surface and many volcanoes. Mars is the planet most like Earth.

Comparing Planets

The four planets farthest from the Sun are called the outer planets. The outer planets are very different from the inner planets. Jupiter, Saturn, Uranus, and Neptune are often called the **gas giants.** They are the largest planets in the solar system and are made up mostly of gases.

Inner and Outer Planets

Planet (in order from Sun)	Diameter	Mass (compared with Earth)	Rings or Moons
Inner Planets			
Mercury	4,879 km (3,032 miles)	0.06 of Earth's mass	None
Venus	12,104 km (7,521 miles)	0.82 of Earth's mass	None
Earth	12,756 km (7,926 miles)	1 Earth	1 Moon
Mars	6,794 km (4,222 miles)	0.11 of Earth's mass	2 Moons
Outer Planets and Pluto			
Jupiter	142,980 km (88,846 miles)	318 Earths	Rings Many moons
Saturn	120,540 km (74,897 miles)	95 Earths	Rings Many moons
Uranus	51,120 km (31,763 miles)	15 Earths	Rings Many moons
Neptune	49,530 km (30,775 miles)	17 Earths	Rings Many moons
Pluto (dwarf planet)	2,390 km (1,485 miles)	less than 0.005 Earth's	1 Moon

Jupiter

Jupiter is the largest planet. In fact, more than 1,000 Earths would fit inside Jupiter. It is so big that all the other planets would fit inside it! A huge storm in Jupiter's atmosphere, called the Great Red Spot, is more than twice the size of Earth. Jupiter rotates so quickly that one day is only 10 hours long.

Like the other gas giants, Jupiter is made up mostly of gases. It is covered by a very deep atmosphere that has high and low clouds. Jupiter's clouds change color daily. They move in bands in opposite directions. Jupiter has at least 63 moons. Scientists think more will be discovered. One of its moons, Io, has active volcanoes on it.

Jupiter	
Composition of Atmosphere	hydrogen and helium
Average Temperature	–74°C (–166°F)
What a 65-Pound Person Would Weigh	about 154 pounds (at cloud-top level)
Distance from Sun Compared with Earth	5 times as far
Interesting Fact	Four of Jupiter's moons can be seen through binoculars.

Great Red Spot

The Great Red Spot has been observed from Earth through telescopes for 300 years.

Alphabet letters are used to name Saturn's rings. The A-ring was discovered in the 1600s when the first telescopes were made.

Saturn

Composition of Atmosphere	hydrogen and helium
Average Temperature	−140°C (−220°F)
What a 65-Pound Person Would Weigh	about 69 pounds (at cloud-top level)
Distance from Sun Compared with Earth	10 times as far
Interesting Fact	Saturn is so light that it could float in water.

Saturn

In 2004 the Cassini spacecraft began sending close-up images of Saturn's bright, beautiful rings. The rings are made of pieces of ice, dust, and rocks. Most pieces are only a few centimeters (about an inch) across. Some are as large as a house. Together the rings are about 282,000 km (175,000 mi) wide, but they are extremely thin.

Saturn is the second largest planet. Like the other gas giants, it is covered by clouds. It also has a small but dense rocky center. Saturn has many moons.

▶ COMPARE AND CONTRAST How are Jupiter and Saturn alike? How are they different?

Uranus

Uranus is the third largest planet. It is only one-third the size of Jupiter. As many as 64 Earths would fit into Uranus, but Earth is much denser than Uranus. Methane, a gas in the planet's atmosphere, gives Uranus its beautiful blue-green color.

Uranus was discovered in 1781 by William Herschel. Its rings are very faint and were not discovered until 1977. Uranus has many moons. Most of them were found by Voyager 2 in 1986. You can find Uranus in the sky with binoculars if you know exactly where to look.

Uranus

Composition of Atmosphere	hydrogen, helium, and methane
Average Temperature	−197°C (−323°F)
What a 65-Pound Person Would Weigh	about 59 pounds
Distance from Sun Compared with Earth	19 times as far
Interesting Fact	Unlike the other planets, Uranus appears to rotate on its side.

Uranus appears to rotate on its side. This unusual tilt may have been caused by a collision with another body in space.

Triton is Neptune's largest moon. The surface of Triton looks somewhat like a cantaloupe. The surface has many geysers.

Neptune	
Composition of Atmosphere	hydrogen, helium, methane
Average Temperature	−200°C (−328°F)
What a 65-Pound Person Would Weigh	about 73 pounds
Distance from Sun Compared with Earth	30 times as far
Interesting Fact	Neptune has a magnetic field that is 25 times stronger than that of Earth.

Neptune

Neptune is the fourth largest planet in the solar system. It is the smallest of the four gas giants. Although it is slightly smaller than Uranus, Neptune has a greater mass. Its diameter is four times larger than Earth's. Neptune is almost 5 billion kilometers (about 3 billion miles) from the Sun.

Neptune has fewer moons than the other gas giants. It has a very active atmosphere. Winds can blow at 1,450 kilometers an hour! Neptune has huge storms. Some of these storms are as big as Earth.

▶ **COMPARE AND CONTRAST** How is Neptune different from the other gas giants?

Pluto, a Dwarf Planet

Pluto was once known as the ninth planet. Today it is classified as a dwarf planet. A dwarf planet is a round, orbiting body much like a planet, but smaller.

Pluto is rocky and icy. The shape of its orbit is an extreme oval, which is tilted compared to the orbits of the planets. As a result, Pluto moves inside of Neptune's orbit once every 248 years.

For many years, scientists have been discussing Pluto and the best way to classify it. Then in 2006, astronomers from around the world met in Prague in the Czech Republic. Most scientists at the meeting agreed that Pluto was too different in size and orbit to be considered a planet.

▶ **COMPARE AND CONTRAST** How is Pluto's orbit different from those of the planets?

Pluto (dwarf planet)

Composition of Atmosphere	nitrogen and methane
Average Temperature	−215°C (−375°F)
What a 65-Pound Person Would Weigh	4.3 pounds
Distance from Sun Compared with Earth	39 times as far
Interesting Fact	Pluto is smaller than some of the moons in the solar system.

Neptune
Pluto

Pluto is only twice as big as its moon, Charon. Even the best photographs of Pluto are blurry and dim because it is so far from Earth.

Lesson Wrap-Up

Visual Summary

Jupiter
- The largest planet
- Made up mostly of gases
- Rings

- An outer planet

Pluto
- The smallest planet
- Rocky and icy
- No rings

LINKS for Home and School

WRITING Story Titan is the largest of the moons of Saturn. In fact, it is larger than either Mercury or Pluto. It also has a thick atmosphere. Learn as much as you can about this moon and write a science fiction story about an expedition to Titan.

MUSIC Describe Music The ancient Greeks imagined that the planets made music as they whirled around the sky. What do you think the music of the planets would sound like? Write a few sentences describing music for each planet. Focus on mood, volume, and high and low pitches. Share your ideas with your classmates.

Review

❶ **MAIN IDEA** List the outer planets in order from nearest to farthest from the Sun.

❷ **VOCABULARY** What is a gas giant?

❸ **READING SKILL: Compare and Contrast** Tell how Jupiter and Pluto are alike and different. Record your ideas in a Venn diagram.

❹ **CRITICAL THINKING: Synthesize** What would you conclude about Pluto—is it a planet or not? Support your conclusion with facts from the lesson.

❺ **INQUIRY SKILL: Measure** Measure and record the diameter, in cm, of each picture of the inner planets shown on D56. Compare the measurements. Which inner planet is smallest?

✓ **TEST PREP**

Which is an outer planet?

A. Mars

B. Earth

C. Saturn

D. Venus

Technology
Visit **www.eduplace.com/scp/** to find out more about the outer planets.

The Solar System Through Time

The earliest humans probably wondered about five bright, wandering spots of light they saw in the sky. The ancient Greeks often referred to them as "wandering stars." In fact, the word *planet* comes from a Greek word that means "wandering." As better tools were invented, people learned more about the solar system.

400 A.D.

1610

1781

Hypatia, a Greek astronomer, used an astrolabe to study and teach. Astronomers used astrolabes until the telescope was invented in the 1600s.

Using a telescope he made, Galileo made observations that supported the idea that the planets revolve around the Sun.

William Herschel discovered the planet Uranus using a 2-m (7-ft) long telescope he designed himself.

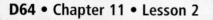

As Earth orbits the Sun, different parts of it are tilted toward the Sun. When the northern half of Earth tilts toward the Sun, it is summer there. Sunlight hits that part of Earth's surface more directly. This causes the temperatures to rise and the period of daylight to be longer.

When the northern half of Earth tilts away from the Sun, it is winter there. Sunlight hits that part of Earth less directly. The temperatures are lower and the period of daylight is shorter.

Changes in the seasons bring changes in the weather. The weather and amount of sunlight affect how plants grow. Plants grow in summer when the period of daylight is long and it is warm. Animals feed on the plants. Many plants die in winter when it is cold. Some animals leave cold areas before the start of winter. They go to warmer places and then return in spring.

▶ **CAUSE AND EFFECT** **What causes summer days to be long and warm?**

Spring

Autumn

about March 21
The northern part of Earth begins tilting toward the Sun.

Winter

Summer

Autumn

about December 22
When the northern part of Earth tilts away from the Sun, it is winter in that part of Earth.

about September 23
The northern part of Earth has stopped tilting toward the Sun and will begin to point away from the Sun.

How the Moon Moves

When you look at the Moon, you always see the same craters and mountains. You see the same features because the same side of the Moon always faces Earth.

Half of the Moon is always lighted by sunlight. But as the Moon orbits Earth, the amount of the lighted side facing Earth changes. These changes produce the phases of the Moon.

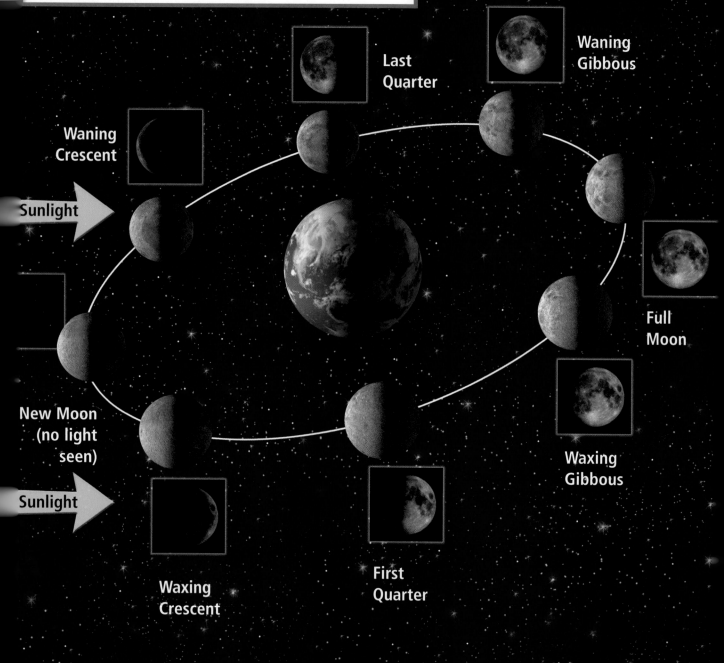

Last Quarter

Waning Gibbous

Waning Crescent

Sunlight

Full Moon

New Moon (no light seen)

Sunlight

Waxing Gibbous

Waxing Crescent

First Quarter

Johann Galle (GO luh), at the Berlin Observatory, was the first to see Neptune.

On July 29, 1969, the Parkes Radio Telescope in Australia provided the best live images of Neil Armstrong walking on the Moon.

A space probe landed on Titan, a moon of Saturn, and sent images of its surface to Earth.

1846   1969   2003 2005

The NASA robot rovers, *Spirit* and *Opportunity*, helped confirm that there was once water on Mars.

Sharing Ideas

1. **READING CHECK** Who discovered the planet Uranus?

2. **WRITE ABOUT IT** What was learned about Mars from *Spirit* and *Opportunity*?

3. **TALK ABOUT IT** How have improvements in technology helped scientists learn more about the Solar System?

How Do Earth and Its Moon Move?

Why It Matters...

The Moon is Earth's nearest neighbor in space. Ancient people watched how the Moon seemed to change each month. They learned to use the Moon as a calendar. In fact, many modern calendars show these changes in the Moon's appearance.

PREPARE TO INVESTIGATE

Inquiry Skill

Experiment When you plan an experiment you have to choose your materials and write a plan that others can follow.

Materials

- flashlight
- baseball
- kickball

Science and Math Toolbox

For step 1, review **Making a Chart to Organize Data** on page H10.

Investigate

Earth-Moon Model

Procedure

1 Collaborate Work with a partner. In your *Science Notebook*, make a chart like the one shown.

2 Place a flashlight at one end of a table pointing to the other end. Do not turn it on yet. Place a kickball on the table in front of the flashlight. Place a baseball on the other side of the kickball so the flashlight and balls are all in a line.

3 Predict Think about how each ball will look when you turn on the flashlight. Work with your partner to predict what you will observe when you turn on the flashlight. Record your prediction.

4 Experiment Turn on the flashlight to check your prediction. Then turn off the flashlight, and record your observations. What you observe is the appearance of a lunar eclipse. A **lunar eclipse** occurs when the Moon passes into Earth's shadow.

5 Turn on the flashlight again. Have your partner slowly roll the baseball from one side of the kickball to the other. Observe and record what happens.

Conclusion

1. Communicate Write a description of how the baseball looked in step 4 compared with how it looked in step 5.

2. Use a Model What part of your model represented the Sun? Earth? Moon?

STEP 1

Position of Baseball	Prediction	Observation
To right of kickball		
To left of kickball		

STEP 2

STEP 4

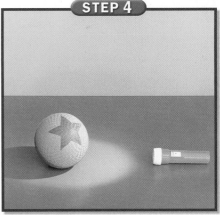

Investigate More!

Design an Experiment As it moves around Earth, the same side of the Moon faces Earth. Design an experiment that models this. Demonstrate your model for your classmates.

Motions of Earth and the Moon

VOCABULARY

axis	p. D68
lunar eclipse	p. D71
phases of the Moon	p. D71
revolution	p. D72
rotation	p. D68

READING SKILL

Cause and Effect Use a chart to show why Earth has different seasons.

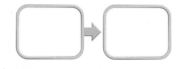

MAIN IDEA The movements of Earth and the Moon cause changes in seasons, daylight hours, the phases of the Moon, and the night sky.

How Earth Moves

Earth makes one complete trip around the Sun in a year. At the start of a new year, Earth is in the same position in relation to the Sun as it was at the start of the year before.

While orbiting the Sun, Earth also turns on an imaginary line called an **axis** (AK sihs). With each **rotation** (roh TAY shuhn), or turn, on Earth's axis, there is one period of daylight and one period of night. Earth's axis is tilted at a 23.5 degree angle from its orbit. The tilt of the Earth on its axis and its orbit around the Sun cause Earth's seasons.

The Seasons

Because Earth's axis is tilted, parts of Earth have four different seasons.

Summer

Winter

about June 21
When the northern part of Earth tilts toward the Sun, it is summer in that part of Earth.

Why does the same side of the Moon always face Earth? Like Earth, the Moon rotates on its axis. The Moon rotates once every 27.3 days. The Moon also orbits Earth once every 27.3 days. Because the two motions take the same amount of time, the same side of the Moon always faces Earth.

You have probably noticed that the Moon seems to change shape from one night to the next. Why? You know that the Moon does not make its own light. Instead, it reflects light from the Sun.

Half of the Moon is nearly always in sunlight. As the Moon orbits Earth, the amount of the lighted side facing Earth changes. These changes produce **phases of the Moon**.

The only time that the Moon is not lighted by sunlight is during a lunar eclipse (LOO nur ih KLIHPS). A **lunar eclipse** occurs when the Moon passes into Earth's shadow. Lunar eclipses occur two to four times a year.

▶ CAUSE AND EFFECT **Why do people on Earth always see the same side of the Moon?**

This picture of a lunar eclipse shows the appearance of the Moon as it moves through Earth's shadow.

During a lunar eclipse, Earth blocks light from the Sun so it cannot strike the Moon. As the Moon moves into Earth's shadow, the shadow seems to move across the Moon.

Sun   Earth   Moon

Rotation and Revolution

Planet	Period of Rotation (in Earth hours or days)	Period of Revolution (in Earth days or years)
Mercury	59 days	87.9 days
Venus	243 days	225 days
Earth	23 hours, 56 minutes	365.25 days
Mars	25 hours	1.88 years
Jupiter	9 hours, 55 minutes	11.86 years
Saturn	10 hours, 40 minutes	29.46 years
Uranus	17 hours, 14 minutes	84 years
Neptune	16 hours, 6 minutes	164.79 years

Comparing Planet Motions

You know that Earth rotates on its axis once each day. The rotation of Earth each day makes the Sun, Moon, stars, and other planets seem to move across the sky.

Like Earth, each planet in the solar system rotates on its axis. But the planets do not rotate at the same speed. The table shows how long it takes for each planet to rotate on its axis. Notice that Earth takes about 24 hours. Some planets take many days to complete one rotation.

All eight planets also orbit the Sun. Each **revolution** (rehv uh LOO-shuhn), or trip around the Sun, is a year. But the length of a year is different for each planet. The table shows that an Earth year is about 365 Earth days. A year on Uranus is about 84 Earth years. That is how long it takes Uranus to make one revolution around the Sun.

▶ **CAUSE AND EFFECT** What causes planets to have days that are longer or shorter than a day on Earth?

Lesson Wrap-Up

Visual Summary

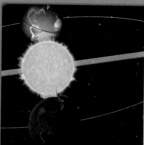
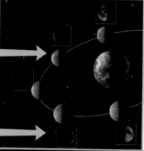

Earth has seasons because of the tilt of its axis. Sunlight shines more directly on half of Earth in summer than in winter.

The phases of the Moon are the changes in the amount of the Moon's lighted side that can be seen from Earth.

The planets rotate on their axes at different rates and revolve around the Sun at different speeds.

 **for Home and School**

MATH **Multiply** It takes Neptune 164.79 years to orbit the Sun. During the time it takes Neptune to make 10 revolutions of the Sun, about how many years will have passed on Earth?

TECHNOLOGY **Model a Rover** The lunar rover had to be lightweight, fold up like a lawn chair, and still haul twice its weight in moon rocks! Find out what challenges the NASA engineers faced when they designed the moon rover. With a partner, construct a model of a moon buggy.

Review

1. **MAIN IDEA** The Sun shines more directly in the northern part of Earth during which season?

2. **VOCABULARY** Write a short paragraph using the term *phases of the Moon*.

3. **READING SKILL: Cause and Effect** Explain why a year on Neptune is much longer than a year on Earth.

4. **CRITICAL THINKING: Analyze** Suppose a new planet were discovered between Jupiter and Saturn. What can you infer about the length of the new planet's year?

5. **INQUIRY SKILL: Experiment** Suppose Earth's axis became more tilted than it already is. How would this affect Earth's seasons? Make a model using a globe and a flashlight to test your ideas.

TEST PREP

The phase of the Moon when none of the lighted side is visible from Earth is called a ___.

A. new moon.

B. full moon.

C. waning crescent.

D. waxing gibbous.

 Technology Visit **www.eduplace.com/scp/** to find out more about Earth and its Moon.

D73

What Are Stars and Galaxies?

Why It Matters...

Stars are so far away that scientists need special equipment to study them. The Hubble Space Telescope and other satellites as well as telescopes on Earth have helped scientists learn about stars and galaxies. This information helps them understand Earth's place in the vastness of space.

PREPARE TO INVESTIGATE

Inquiry Skill

Observe When you observe, you gather information about the environment using your five senses: seeing, hearing, smelling, touching, and tasting.

Materials

- star clock Activity Support Master
- scissors
- paper fastener

Science and Math Toolbox

For step 1, review **Making a Chart to Organize Data** on page H10.

Star Clock

Procedure

1. In your *Science Notebook*, make a chart like the one shown.

2. Cut out the Star Clock base and the Star Clock wheel. Place the wheel on top of the base. Attach the two parts by pushing a paper fastener through the center of each. **Safety:** Be careful. The paper fastener is sharp.

3. **Collaborate** Work with a partner. Discuss the times given on the base of the clock. Note how this is different from a time clock.

4. **Use Models** Turn the wheel so that the Big Dipper is at the left. Find March and read and record the time for mid-March. That is the time when the Big Dipper will be in that position in the sky.

5. **Record Data** Turn the wheel so the Big Dipper is at the top, to the right, and then to the bottom. For each position, read and record the times for mid-March.

6. Follow steps 4 and 5 to complete your chart for the other three months.

Conclusion

1. **Observe** How does the position of the North Star change during the night?

2. **Infer** How could people use the pattern of the Big Dipper's movement to tell time?

STEP 1

Position of Big Dipper	March	June	Sept.	Dec.
Left				
Top				
Bottom				
Right				

STEP 2

STEP 5

Investigate More!

Design an Experiment
Use your star chart at home with an adult family member. Find the Big Dipper and North Star. Use your star clock to find the time.

VOCABULARY

constellation	p. D78
galaxy	p. D79
star	p. D76
universe	p. D79

READING SKILL

Main Idea and Details
Use a chart to list details about the universe.

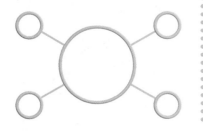

Stars and Galaxies

MAIN IDEA The universe is made up of all the stars, galaxies, planets, and moons in space.

The Sun and Other Stars

When you see stars twinkling in the night sky, do you ever wonder what stars are made of? A **star** is a huge ball of very hot gases that gives off light, heat, and other kinds of energy. Some of the ways stars can be classified are by their size, color, brightness, and temperature. Stars can shine for billions of years.

The Sun is a star that is both medium in its size and in its brightness. Many other stars are larger and brighter. Why does the Sun look so much larger and brighter than any other star? The reason is that the Sun is much closer to Earth than any other star. Light from the Sun takes 8 minutes to reach Earth. Light from the next nearest star takes over 4 years to reach Earth.

MAIN IDEA Why does the Sun appear brighter and larger than other stars?

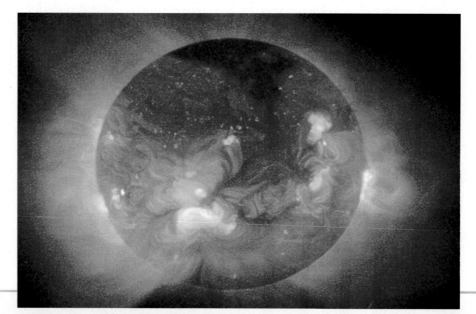

The Sun's energy has been giving Earth light and heat for 4.5 billion years. ▶

Kinds of Stars

Stars are classified by color as blue, blue-white, white, yellow, orange-red, and red. Scientists also classify stars by their size, brightness, and temperature.

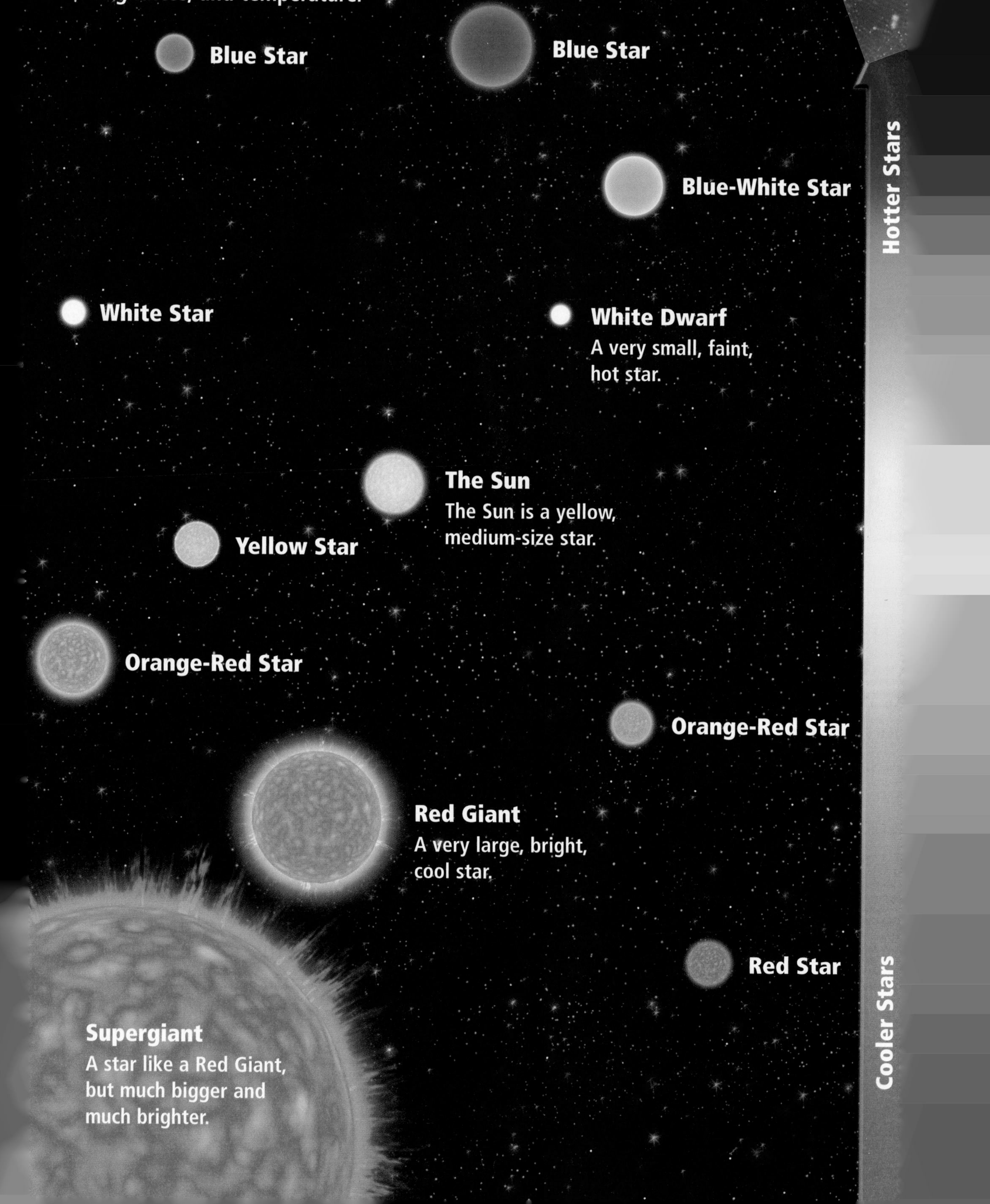

Blue Star

Blue Star

Blue-White Star

White Star

White Dwarf
A very small, faint, hot star.

The Sun
The Sun is a yellow, medium-size star.

Yellow Star

Orange-Red Star

Orange-Red Star

Red Giant
A very large, bright, cool star.

Red Star

Supergiant
A star like a Red Giant, but much bigger and much brighter.

Hotter Stars

Cooler Stars

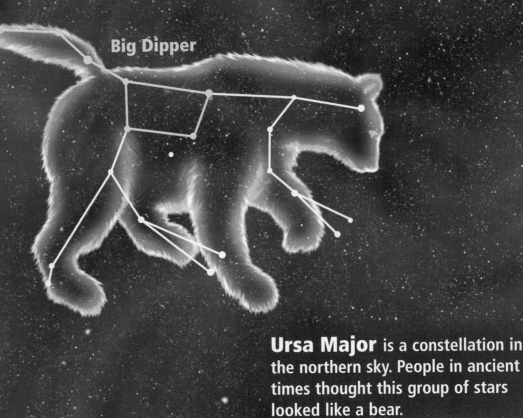

Big Dipper

Ursa Major is a constellation in the northern sky. People in ancient times thought this group of stars looked like a bear.

Constellations

Have you ever looked up at clouds and thought that they looked like objects or animals? Perhaps you have seen pictures in groups of stars. Throughout history, people have made up stories about the pictures they imagined were formed by groups of stars.

A **constellation** (KAHN stuh lay-shuhn) is a group of stars that forms a pattern in the night sky. One well-known constellation is Ursa Major (UR suh MAY jur), which means "Great Bear." Some of the stars in Ursa Major make up another group of stars called the Big Dipper.

Have you ever viewed a bright star early in the evening? If you look for it again later that night, it will be in a different position. The stars do not actually move. They appear to because Earth is rotating. As Earth rotates on its axis, you see different parts of the sky. The stars appear to move across the sky during the night. The stars are in the sky during the day as well. But the brightness of sunlight makes it impossible for you to see them.

Galaxies

You know that the Sun, the planets, and the moons are part of the solar system. But did you know that the solar system is part of a larger group? It is part of a galaxy (GAL uhk see). A **galaxy** is a huge system, or group, of stars held together by gravity.

The solar system is located in a galaxy called the Milky Way. The Milky Way Galaxy is spiral-shaped. Scientists classify galaxies into three types by their shape: spiral, oval or round, and irregular.

The **universe** (YOO nuh vurs) is made up of all the matter and energy there is, including all the galaxies, and their stars, planets, and moons. There are billions of galaxies in the universe. The size of the universe is unknown. Scientists believe that it is expanding, or growing outward in every direction.

▶ **MAIN IDEA**   What is a galaxy?

Milky Way Galaxy

Location of
Solar System

The stars and planets that you see at night are in the
Milky Way Galaxy. How would you describe the shape

Visual Summary

A star is a huge ball of extremely hot gases. Stars can be classified by their size, color, temperature, and age.

A constellation is a group of stars that forms a pattern, or picture, in the night sky.

A galaxy is a huge group of stars held together by gravity. The universe is made up of all the galaxies and objects in space.

LINKS for Home and School

MATH Classify Shapes Use a star chart to examine some constellations. Break the constellations down into basic geometric shapes such as triangles, trapezoids, and hexagons. Classify the shapes using geometry terms you have learned. Sketch the constellation using colors or shading to indicate the shapes.

WRITING Story Choose a constellation such as Ursa Major or make up a constellation of your own. Write a story about how the animal, object, or person came to be a constellation.

Review

1 MAIN IDEA What objects can be found in a galaxy?

2 VOCABULARY Write a sentence about the universe. Be sure to use the terms *galaxy* and *stars*.

3 READING SKILL: Main Idea and Details Choose one of the headings in the lesson to serve as a main idea. Write details that support that main idea.

4 CRITICAL THINKING: Apply Use the picture on page D77 of the star types. Which would be hottest: a blue-white star, an orange-red star, or a yellow star?

5 INQUIRY SKILL: Observe Choose a picture of a star, constellation, or galaxy from this lesson. Study the picture carefully. Write a detailed description of what you see.

✓ TEST PREP

A constellation is a ____.

A. young, growing star.

B. ball of extremely hot gases that gives off energy.

C. group, or system, of stars held together by gravity.

D. group of stars that forms a pattern in the night sky.

Technology
Visit **www.eduplace.com/scp/** to find out more about stars and galaxies.

Meteorologist

Some meteorologists broadcast weather reports on television. But most work behind the scenes at national and international weather stations. Meteorologists rely on weather satellites and weather radar to collect and analyze data. Computers help them use this data to make forecasts.

What It Takes!

- A degree in meteorology or atmospheric science
- Math and computer skills; interest in chemistry, physics, and earth science

Environmental Science and Protection Technicians

Environmental science and protection technicians help monitor pollution. During one week, they might collect samples of air, water, or soil. The next week, they might help analyze those samples in a lab. People in this job often must oversee the proper disposal of hazardous wastes.

What It Takes!

- A high-school diploma
- Courses in applied science or science-related technology
- Strong math, computer, and communications skills

BLASTS from the SUN

Did someone say big? The Sun is so big, and so powerful, that next to it the biggest explosion on earth seems puny. So when the Sun itself erupts with a sudden blast of energy, you know it's going to be extreme.

This picture shows what is called an eruptive prominence. It is one of several types of solar bursts that can affect Earth. When one occurs, a huge portion of the Sun is literally ejected into outer space. The speed of these eruptions can reach millions of miles an hour!

When the high-speed, high-energy particles of a solar eruption reach Earth, they light up the night sky with fantastic, colorful auroras. The most powerful solar eruptions can create electrical surges in power networks, causing blackouts for millions of people.

Solar eruptions are so big they can be measured in terms of Earth itself. How many Earths long is this eruption?

Vocabulary

Complete each sentence with a term from the list.

1. The different shapes of the Moon when viewed from Earth are the _____.

2. Earth rotates on its _____.

3. The Sun is at the center of the _____.

4. All the objects in space, including the Milky Way and other galaxies, make up the _____.

5. The Moon moves into the shadow of Earth during a/an _____.

6. The Sun is a medium-sized _____.

7. A group of stars that forms a picture or pattern in the night sky is a/an _____.

8. The cycle of day and night is caused by Earth's _____.

9. Because of their size and the materials that make them up, Jupiter, Saturn, Uranus, and Neptune are called the _____.

10. The planets are kept in orbit around the Sun by _____.

axis D68
constellation D78
galaxy D79
gas giants D57
gravity D52
lunar eclipse D71
orbit D50
phases of the Moon D71
planet D50
revolution D72
rotation D68
solar system D50
star D76
universe D79

Test Prep

Write the letter of the best answer choice.

11. What is a galaxy?

   A. all the planets that orbit the Sun
   B. all the objects in the universe
   C. a large group of stars held together by gravity
   D. a group of stars that forms a pattern, or picture, in the night sky

12. Earth travels around the Sun along a path called a(n) _____.

   A. rotation   **C.** eclipse
   B. orbit   **D.** axis

13. A large body that travels in an orbit around the Sun is a _____.

   A. star
   B. planet
   C. galaxy
   D. constellation

14. It takes 365 days for Earth to make one _____ of the Sun.

   A. rotation   **C.** revolution
   B. axis   **D.** constellation

15. Collaborate Work with a partner. Discuss what you think would happen if the Sun did not shine on Earth. Make a list of your ideas.

16. Observe One orbit of the Moon begins with a new Moon and ends with a new Moon. What is the phase of the Moon when it is halfway around its orbit?

Map the Concept

The Venn diagram compares the solar system and the Milky Way Galaxy. Place the descriptions below in their appropriate place in the diagram.

It is shaped like a spiral.
There are many stars in it.
There are only eight planets in it.
Gravity holds the parts together.
There is only one star, the Sun, in it.
All the objects in the solar system are in it.

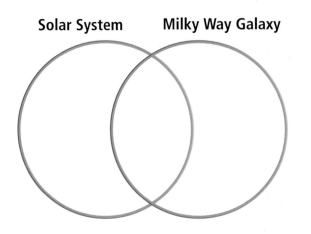

Solar System   Milky Way Galaxy

Critical Thinking

17. Synthesize If the Moon started rotating faster than it does now, what would be different about how the Moon looks from Earth? Explain your answer.

18. Evaluate Someone tells you that Earth's Moon produces its own light. He says that the proof of this is that the Moon is very bright at night. Evaluate this statement.

19. Analyze How are the solar system, the Milky Way, and the universe related?

20. Apply Sophie observed the positions of the Big Dipper and North Star in different seasons. Study her observations in the table. What do you think her data will show for spring? Explain.

Season	Position of Big Dipper at 8:30 P.M.
Summer	to the left
Autumn	below
Winter	to the right

Performance Assessment

Model the Size of the Sun
Use your thumb and a door to model how distance affects apparent size. Stretch your arm out and hold your thumb up. Look past your thumb at a door. Which looks bigger? Now move your thumb close to your nose and look past it at the same door. Which looks bigger now? Use this model to explain why the Sun looks bigger than other stars.

Write the letter of the best answer choice.

1. Which gas makes up the largest portion of Earth's atmosphere?

   A. water
   B. oxygen
   C. carbon dioxide
   D. nitrogen

2. When a warm front moves into a region, it usually brings _____.

   A. hot, dry air.
   B. warm, dry air.
   C. gray clouds and rain.
   D. violent thunderstorms.

3. What is shown in the picture?

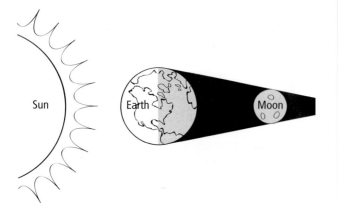

   A. new moon
   B. lunar eclipse
   C. full moon
   D. gibbous moon

4. Which planet is NOT a large ball of gas?

   A. Jupiter
   B. Venus
   C. Saturn
   D. Uranus

5. The diagram below shows the movement of air during the day. Which labels go with arrow 1 and arrow 2?

   A. arrow 1—Cool Air
      arrow 2—Cool Air
   B. arrow 1—Cool Air
      arrow 2—Warm Air
   C. arrow 1—Warm Air
      arrow 2—Cool Air
   D. arrow 1—Warm Air,
      arrow 2—Warm Air

6. Which type of star is the hottest?

   A. blue star
   B. supergiant
   C. white dwarf
   D. yellow star

7. Which climate zone has warm, dry summers and cold, wet winters?

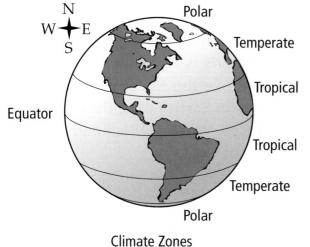

Climate Zones

A. polar
B. temperate
C. tropical
D. Equator

8. Which part of the water cycle is shown?

A. condensation
B. evaporation
C. precipitation
D. rotation

Answer the following in complete sentences.

9. A friend tells you that Austin, Texas, has a warm, temperate climate. You visit Austin in January and it is very cold. Was your friend wrong? Explain.

10. The same side of the Moon always faces Earth. Does the Sun ever shine on the side we cannot see? Explain your answer.

As Earth rotates on its axis all stars except for Polaris appear to move across the sky in circular paths. Polaris is also called the North Star because it lies almost directly above the North Pole. Since the North Pole and the South Pole form Earth's axis, they do not move as the rest of Earth rotates. The North Star is lined up with the axis, so it appears to stay still as well.

As Earth rotates on its axis, your view of the sky constantly changes. The Big Dipper and other stars appear to revolve around Polaris because Polaris is in line with Earth's axis.

You can locate Polaris in the sky by looking for the Big Dipper. Two stars in the Big Dipper point to Polaris.

See how the stars move in the sky around Polaris as Earth turns. Go to **www.eduplace.com/scp/** to learn more about the North Star.

Science and Math Toolbox

Using a Hand Lens H2

Making a Bar Graph H3

Using a Calculator H4

Finding an Average H5

Using a Tape Measure or Ruler H6

Measuring Volume H7

Using a Thermometer H8

Using a Balance H9

Making a Chart to Organize Data H10

Reading a Circle Graph H11

Measuring Elapsed Time H12

Measurements H14

Using a Hand Lens

A hand lens is a tool that magnifies objects, or makes objects appear larger. This makes it possible for you to see details of an object that would be hard to see without the hand lens.

Look at a Coin or a Stamp

1 Place an object such as a coin or a stamp on a table or other flat surface.

STEP 1

2 Hold the hand lens just above the object. As you look through the lens, slowly move the lens away from the object. Notice that the object appears to get larger and a little blurry.

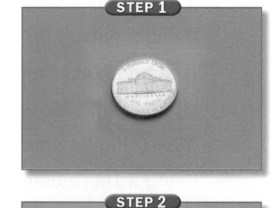

STEP 2

3 Move the hand lens a little closer to the object until the object is once again in sharp focus.

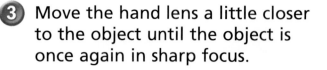

STEP 3

Making a Bar Graph

A bar graph helps you organize and compare data.

Make a Bar Graph of Animal Heights

Animals come in all different shapes and sizes. You can use the information in this table to make a bar graph of animal heights.

1 Draw the side and the bottom of the graph. Label the side of the graph as shown. The numbers will show the height of the animals in centimeters.

2 Label the bottom of the graph. Write the names of the animals at the bottom so that there is room to draw the bars.

3 Choose a title for your graph. Your title should describe the subject of the graph.

4 Draw bars to show the height of each animal. Some heights are between two numbers.

Heights of Animals

Animal	Height (cm)
Bear	240
Elephant	315
Cow	150
Giraffe	570
Camel	210
Horse	165

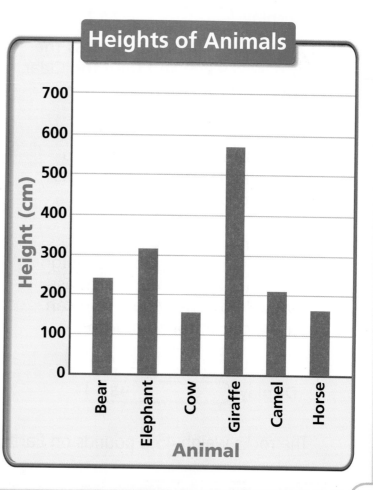

Heights of Animals

Using a Calculator

After you've made measurements, a calculator can help you analyze your data.

Add and Multiply Decimals

Suppose you're an astronaut. You may take 8 pounds of Moon rocks back to Earth. Can you take all the rocks in the table? Use a calculator to find out.

Weight of Moon Rocks

Moon Rock	Weight of Rock on Moon (lb)
Rock 1	1.7
Rock 2	1.8
Rock 3	2.6
Rock 4	1.5

 To add, press:

[1] [.] [7] [+] [1] [.] [8] [+]
[2] [.] [6] [+] [1] [.] [5] [=]

Display: [7.6]

2 If you make a mistake, press the left arrow key and then the Clear key. Enter the number again. Then continue adding.

3 Your total is 7.6 pounds. You can take the four Moon rocks back to Earth.

4 How much do the Moon rocks weigh on Earth? Objects weigh six times as much on Earth as they do on the Moon. You can use a calculator to multiply.

Press: [7] [.] [6] [×] [6] [=]

Display: [45.6]

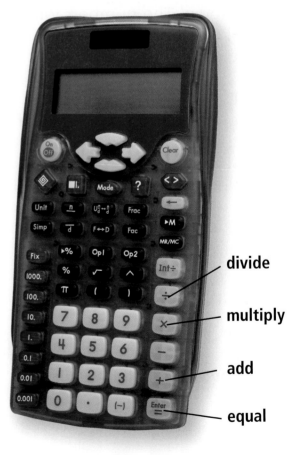

divide

multiply

add

equal

The rocks weigh 45.6 pounds on Earth.

Finding an Average

An average is a way to describe a group of numbers. For example, after you have made a series of measurements, you can find the average. This can help you analyze your data.

Add and Divide to Find the Average

The table shows the amount of rain that fell each month for the first six months of the year. What was the average rainfall per month?

1 Add the numbers in the list.

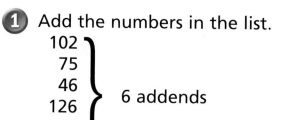

$$\left.\begin{array}{r} 102 \\ 75 \\ 46 \\ 126 \\ 51 \\ + \ 32 \\ \hline 432 \end{array}\right\} \text{6 addends}$$

2 Divide the sum (432) by the number of addends (6).

$$\begin{array}{r} 72 \\ 6\overline{)432} \\ -\ 42 \\ \hline 12 \\ -\ 12 \\ \hline 0 \end{array}$$

Rainfall	
Month	**Rain (mm)**
January	102
February	75
March	46
April	126
May	51
June	32

The average rainfall per month for the first six months was 72 mm of rain.

Using a Tape Measure or Ruler

Tape measures and rulers are tools for measuring the length of objects and distances. Scientists most often use units such as meters, centimeters, and millimeters when making length measurements.

Use a Tape Measure

1 Measure the distance around a jar. Wrap the tape around the jar.

2 Find the line where the tape begins to wrap over itself.

3 Record the distance around the jar to the nearest centimeter.

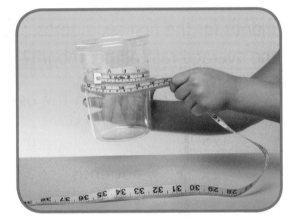

Use a Metric Ruler

1 Measure the length of your shoe. Place the ruler or the meterstick on the floor. Line up the end of the ruler with the heel of your shoe.

2 Notice where the other end of your shoe lines up with the ruler.

3 Look at the scale on the ruler. Record the length of your shoe to the nearest centimeter and to the nearest millimeter.

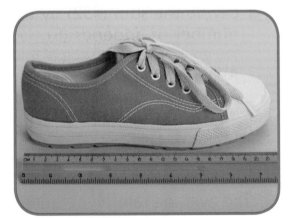

Measuring Volume

A beaker, a measuring cup, and a graduated cylinder are used to measure volume. Volume is the amount of space something takes up. Most of the containers that scientists use to measure volume have a scale marked in milliliters (mL).

**Beaker
50 mL**   **Measuring cup
50 mL**   **Graduated
cylinder
50 mL**

Measure the Volume of a Liquid

1 Measure the volume of juice. Pour some juice into a measuring container.

2 Move your head so that your eyes are level with the top of the juice. Read the scale line that is closest to the surface of the juice. If the surface of the juice is curved up on the sides, look at the lowest point of the curve.

3 Read the measurement on the scale. You can estimate the value between two lines on the scale.

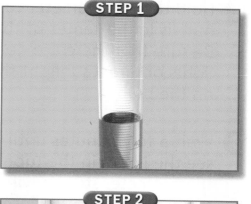

STEP 1

STEP 2

Using a Thermometer

A thermometer is used to measure temperature. When the liquid in the tube of a thermometer gets warmer, it expands and moves farther up the tube. Different scales can be used to measure temperature, but scientists usually use the Celsius scale.

Measure the Temperature of a Liquid

1 Half fill a cup with warm tap water.

2 Hold the thermometer so that the bulb is in the center of the liquid. Be sure that there are no bright lights or direct sunlight shining on the bulb.

3 Wait a few minutes until you see the liquid in the tube of the thermometer stop moving. Read the scale line that is closest to the top of the liquid in the tube. The thermometer shown reads 22°C (72°F).

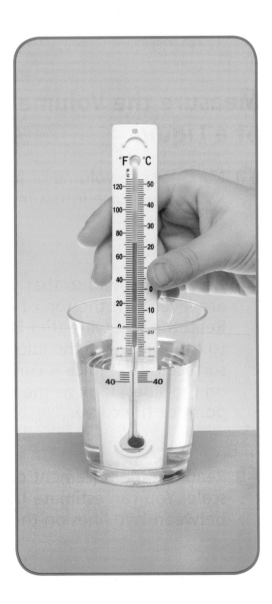

Using a Balance

A balance is used to measure mass. Mass is the amount of matter in an object. To find the mass of an object, place it in the left pan of the balance. Place standard masses in the right pan.

Measure the Mass of a Ball

1 Check that the empty pans are balanced, or level with each other. When balanced, the pointer on the base should be at the middle mark. If it needs to be adjusted, move the slider on the back of the balance a little to the left or right.

2 Place a ball on the left pan. Then add standard masses, one at a time, to the right pan. When the pointer is at the middle mark again, each pan holds the same amount of matter and has the same mass.

3 Add the numbers marked on the masses in the pan. The total is the mass of the ball in grams.

Making a Chart to Organize Data

A chart can help you keep track of information. When you organize information, or data, it is easier to read, compare, or classify it.

Classifying Animals

Suppose you want to organize this data about animal characteristics. You could base the chart on the two characteristics listed—the number of wings and the number of legs.

1 Give the chart a title that describes the data in it.

2 Name categories, or groups, that describe the data you have collected.

3 Make sure the information is recorded correctly in each column.

Next, you could make another chart to show animal classification based on number of legs only.

My Data

Fleas have no wings. Fleas have six legs.

Snakes have no wings or legs.

A bee has four wings. It has six legs.

Spiders never have wings. They have eight legs.

A dog has no wings. It has four legs.

Birds have two wings and two legs.

A cow has no wings. It has four legs.

A butterfly has four wings. It has six legs.

Animals–Number of Wings and Legs

Animal	Number of Wings	Number of Legs
Flea	0	6
Snake	0	0
Bee	4	6
Spider	0	8
Dog	0	4
Bird	2	2
Butterfly	4	6

Reading a Circle Graph

A circle graph shows a whole divided into parts. You can use a circle graph to compare the parts to each other. You can also use it to compare the parts to the whole.

A Circle Graph of Fuel Use

This circle graph shows fuel use in the United States. The graph has 10 equal parts, or sections. Each section equals $\frac{1}{10}$ of the whole. One whole equals $\frac{10}{10}$.

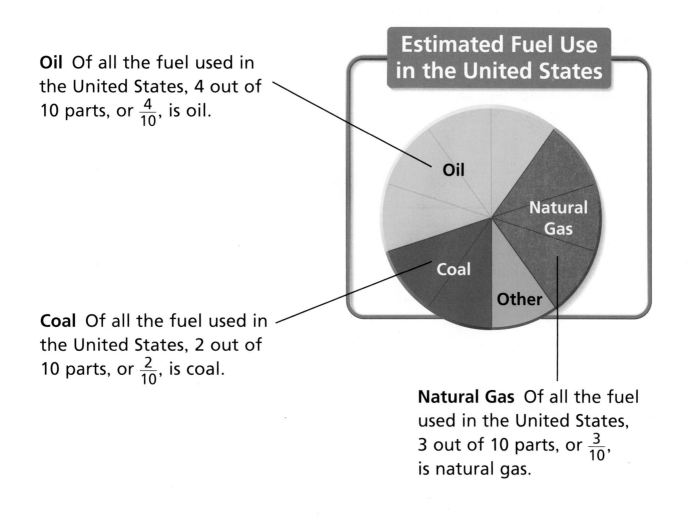

Oil Of all the fuel used in the United States, 4 out of 10 parts, or $\frac{4}{10}$, is oil.

Coal Of all the fuel used in the United States, 2 out of 10 parts, or $\frac{2}{10}$, is coal.

Natural Gas Of all the fuel used in the United States, 3 out of 10 parts, or $\frac{3}{10}$, is natural gas.

Estimated Fuel Use in the United States

Oil

Natural Gas

Coal

Other

Measuring Elapsed Time

A calendar can help you find out how much time has passed, or elapsed, in days or weeks. A clock can help you see how much time has elapsed in hours and minutes. A clock with a second hand or a stopwatch can help you find out how many seconds have elapsed.

Using a Calendar to Find Elapsed Days

This is a calendar for the month of October. October has 31 days. Suppose it is October 22 and you begin an experiment. You need to check the experiment two days from the start date and one week from the start date. That means you would check it on Wednesday, October 24, and again on Monday, October 29. October 29 is 7 days after October 22.

Days of the Week
Monday, Tuesday, Wednesday, Thursday, and Friday are weekdays. Saturday and Sunday are weekends.

Last Month
Last month ended on Sunday, September 30.

October

Sunday	Monday	Tuesday	Wednesday	Thursday	Friday	Saturday
	1	2	3	4	5	6
7	8	9	10	11	12	13
14	15	16	17	18	19	20
21	22	23	24	25	26	27
28	29	30	31			

Next Month
Next month begins on Thursday, November 1.

Using a Clock or a Stopwatch to Find Elapsed Time

You need to time an experiment for 20 minutes.

It is 1:30 P.M.

Stop at 1:50 P.M.

You need to time an experiment for 15 seconds. You can use the second hand of a clock or watch.

Start the experiment when the second hand is on number 6.

Stop when 15 seconds have passed and the second hand is on the 9.

You can use a stopwatch to time 15 seconds.

Press the reset button on a stopwatch so that you see 0:00 00.

Press the start button. When you see 0:15 00, press the stop button.

Measurements

Volume

1 L of sports drink is a little more than 1 qt.

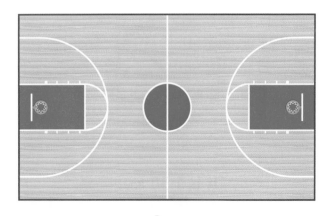

Area

A basketball court covers about 4,700 ft². It covers about 435 m².

Metric Measures

Temperature

- Ice melts at 0 degrees Celsius (°C)
- Water freezes at 0°C
- Water boils at 100°C

Length and Distance

- 1,000 meters (m) = 1 kilometer (km)
- 100 centimeters (cm) = 1 m
- 10 millimeters (mm) = 1 cm

Force

- 1 newton (N) = 1 kilogram × 1 (meter/second) per second

Volume

- 1 cubic meter (m³) = 1 m × 1 m × 1 m
- 1 cubic centimeter (cm³) = 1 cm × 1 cm × 1 cm
- 1 liter (L) = 1,000 milliliters (mL)
- 1 cm³ = 1 mL

Area

- 1 square kilometer (km²) = 1 km × 1 km
- 1 hectare = 10,000 m²

Mass

- 1,000 grams (g) = 1 kilogram (kg)
- 1,000 milligrams (mg) = 1 g

Temperature

The temperature at an indoor basketball game might be 27°C, which is 80°F.

Length and Distance

A basketball rim is about 10 ft high, or a little more than 3 m from the floor.

Customary Measures

Temperature

- Ice melts at 32 degrees Fahrenheit (°F)
- Water freezes at 32°F
- Water boils at 212°F

Length and Distance

- 12 inches (in.) = 1 foot (ft)
- 3 ft = 1 yard (yd)
- 5,280 ft = 1 mile (mi)

Weight

- 16 ounces (oz) = 1 pound (lb)
- 2,000 pounds = 1 ton (T)

Volume of Fluids

- 8 fluid ounces (fl oz) = 1 cup (c)
- 2 c = 1 pint (pt)
- 2 pt = 1 quart (qt)
- 4 qt = 1 gallon (gal)

Metric and Customary Rates

km/h = kilometers per hour

m/s = meters per second

mph = miles per hour

Health and Fitness Handbook

Being healthy means that all parts of your body and mind work well together. To keep your body healthy,

- know how to take care of your body systems.
- use safe behaviors when you play.
- choose the right amounts of healthful foods.
- get physical activity every day.
- use behaviors that keep you well.

This handbook will help you learn ways to keep yourself healthy and safe. What will *you* do to stay healthy?

The Nervous System H18
Your nervous system controls your body.

A Nerve Cell H19
Learn how nerve cells carry messages.

Safety in Every Season H20
Find tips to help you stay safe outdoors.

The Exercise Cycle H21
Learn the three parts of a good exercise plan.

Servings for Good Nutrition H22
Find out how many servings to eat of
different kinds of food.

Stop Diseases From Spreading H23
Do you know how to avoid spreading germs? Find out.

The Nervous System

Central Nervous System

Brain The brain is the control center for the body.

Spinal Cord The spinal cord is a bundle of nerves that extends down your back.

- Messages to and from the brain travel through the spinal cord.
- Sometimes the spinal cord sends messages directly to other nerves without sending them to the brain first.

brain

spinal cord

Peripheral Nervous System

Peripheral means "on the outside." Peripheral nerves connect the brain and spinal cord to the rest of the body. There are two kinds of peripheral nerves.

Sensory Nerves These nerves carry messages *to* the central nervous system.

Motor Nerves These nerves carry messages *from* the central nervous system.

The nervous system carries millions of messages every minute. These messages tell you:

- what you see, hear, taste, smell, and touch.
- what you think and how you feel.
- how your body is working.

A Nerve Cell

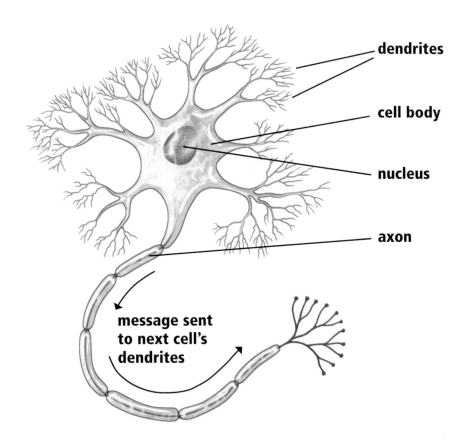

dendrites

cell body

nucleus

axon

message sent to next cell's dendrites

Nerve cells are called *neurons.* They carry messages to and from the brain and spinal cord. You are born with almost all the neurons your body will ever form. Here's an example of how neurons work.

1 You touch something hot. Cells in your fingertips send a warning message.

2 Dendrites in cells in your sensory nerves pick up the message. They send it to other neurons through their axons.

3 The message reaches the spinal cord.

4 The spinal cord sends messages to motor nerves. The messages cause the muscles in your hand to move away from the hot object.

All of this happens in less time than it takes you to blink!

Safety in Every Season

Being outside in all kinds of weather can be fun! But to be safe, you need to pay attention.

Hot Weather

Protect your skin from the harmful rays of the Sun.

- Always wear sunscreen with a SPF of at least 15.
- Wear sunglasses that protect against UVA and UVB rays.
- Loose-fitting clothes keep you cool and protect your skin. A hat helps, too!
- Drink plenty of water.

Cold Weather

Dress for cold weather in warm layers.

- Wear a hat, gloves or mittens, and socks.
- A waterproof outer layer is a good idea.
- Wear sunscreen. Bright sunlight can reflect from snow and ice.

Water Safety

When swimming:
- always have a buddy.
- know your limits.
- rest often.

Ice Safety

When walking on ice:
- tilt your body forward.
- set your feet down flat.
- take short steps.

Poisonous Plants

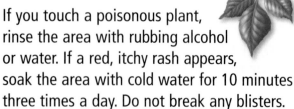

If you touch a poisonous plant, rinse the area with rubbing alcohol or water. If a red, itchy rash appears, soak the area with cold water for 10 minutes three times a day. Do not break any blisters.

Stinging Insects

Remove the insect's stinger by scraping it with something stiff, like a credit card. Make a paste of baking soda and water. Apply it to the place where the stinger was. Use a cold pack to help reduce itching and swelling.

The Exercise Cycle

Physical activity is important for good health. It makes your heart, lungs, and muscles strong. It helps you keep a healthful weight, too. It's best to get physical activity every day. When you exercise, include a warm-up, exercise, and a cool-down.

1 **Warm-up** Begin with five minutes of gentle activity. Walking is a good way to warm up your body. Also stretch your muscles gently. This helps prevent injury.

2 **Exercise** Exercise at a steady level for 20 minutes. You should feel your heart beating faster. You should also be breathing hard, but not so hard that you couldn't talk to a friend at the same time.

3 **Cool-down** Exercise at a lower level for about five minutes. Your heart rate and breathing should slow down. Then spend five more minutes stretching your muscles again.

Tips

✔ Drink extra water before, during, and after exercise. This replaces water your body loses when you sweat.

✔ If you are injured or an exercise hurts when you do it, stop right away and tell an adult.

Servings for Good Nutrition

Food gives you energy. It also provides materials your body needs to grow and develop. It's important to eat the right kinds of food in the right amounts and to get physical activity. Together, these will help you maintain a healthful weight.

Food Group	Daily Amount	Examples
Grains	3–6 oz.	bread cereal cooked rice or pasta
Vegetables	2–4 cups	leafy vegetables chopped vegetables, cooked or raw vegetable juice
Fruits	1–2 cups	apple, banana, or orange chopped, cooked, or canned fruit
Milk	2–3 cups	milk or yogurt natural cheese processed cheese
Meat and Beans	5$\frac{1}{2}$ oz.	cooked lean meat, poultry, or fish beans nuts

Stop Diseases From Spreading

Sometimes when you're ill, you have a contagious disease. *Contagious* means that you can spread the illness to others. These diseases are caused by harmful bacteria or viruses that enter the body.

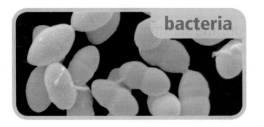

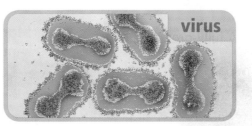

Bacteria cause...
- tetanus
- food poisoning
- strep throat

Viruses cause...
- the common cold
- the flu
- measles
- mumps
- chicken pox

To help stop the spread of these diseases, stay home when you are ill. Also do these things:

- Cover your mouth and nose when you sneeze or cough.
- Throw away tissues after you use them.
- Wash your hands often during the day.
- Keep wounds clean and covered.

❖ The Best Recipe for Disease Prevention ❖

Eat healthful foods and handle food safely.

Exercise every day.

Get plenty of sleep.

Keep your body clean.

Have regular check-ups with your doctor and dentist.

Glossary

A

adaptation (ad ap TAY shuhn) A physical feature or a behavior that helps an organism survive in its habitat. (B60)

adult (uh DUHLT) A fully-grown, mature organism. (A71)

air mass (air mas) A large body of air that has about the same temperature, air pressure, and moisture throughout. (D25)

air pressure (air PRESH uhr) The weight of air as it presses down on Earth's surface. (D8)

analyze data (AN uh lyz DAY tuh) To look for patterns in collected information that lead to making logical inferences, predictions, and hypotheses.

artery (AHR tuh ree) Any blood vessel that carries blood away from the heart to capillaries. (A42)

ask questions (ask KWEHS chuhz) To state orally or in writing questions to find out how or why something happens, which can lead to scientific investigations or research.

atmosphere (AT muh sfihr) The layers of air that surround Earth's surface. (D8)

atom (AT uhm) The smallest particle of matter that has the properties of that matter. (E7)

axis (AK sihs) An imaginary line through the center of an object. (D68)

B

behavior (bih HAYV yur) The way that an organism acts or responds to its environment. (A100)

biodegradable (by oh dih GRAY duh buhl) Able to break down easily in the environment. (C62)

blood (bludh) The substance that carries nutrients and oxygen to every cell in the body. (A36)

C

camouflage (KAM uh flazh) The coloring, marking, or other physical appearance of an animal that helps it blend in with its surroundings. (B62)

capillary (KAP uh layr ee) A tiny blood vessel that connects arteries and veins. (A42)

carnivore (KAHR nuh vawr) An animal that eats only other animals. (B38)

cell (sehl) The basic unit that makes up all living things. (A8)

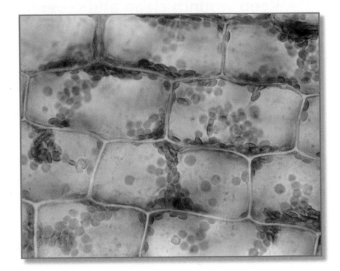

chemical change (KEHM ih kuhl chaynj) A change in matter that produces new kinds of matter with different properties. (E66)

chemical property (KEHM ih kuhl PRAP ur tee) A characteristic of matter that can be observed only when matter is changed into a new kind of matter. (E27)

chemical reaction (KEHM ih kuhl ree AK shuhn) Another term for a chemical change. (E67)

chlorophyll (KLAWR uh fihl) A green material in plants that traps energy from sunlight and gives leaves their green color. (A22)

circulatory system (SUR kyuh luh tawr ee SIHS tuhm) The system that transports oxygen, nutrients, and wastes. (A42)

classify (KLAS uh fy) To sort objects into groups according to their properties or order objects according to a pattern.

climate (KLY muht) The average weather conditions in an area over a long period of time. (D34)

collaborate (kuh LAB uh rayt) To work as a team with others to collect and share data, observations, findings, and ideas.

communicate (kah MYOO nuh kayt) To explain procedures or share information, data, or findings with others through written or spoken words, actions, graphs, charts, tables, diagrams, or sketches.

community (kuh MYOO nih tee) All the organisms that live in the same ecosystem and interact with each other. (B12)

compare (kuhm PAIR) To observe and tell how objects or events are alike or different.

condensation (kahn dehn SAY shuhn) The change of the state of gas to a liquid. (C42, D15)

conduction (kuhn DUHK shuhn) The transfer of thermal energy from particle to particle between two objects that are touching. (F32)

conductors (kuhn DUHK tuhrz) Materials that negatively charged particles can move through easily. (F55)

conservation (kahn sur VAY shuhn) The preserving and wise use of natural resources. (C61)

constellation (KAHN stuh lay shuhn) A group of stars that forms a pattern in the night sky. (D78)

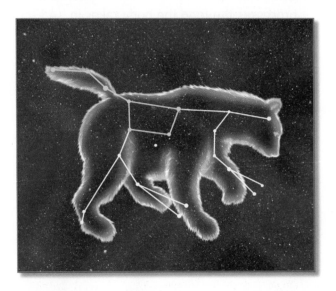

consumer (kuhn SOO mur) An organism that eats other living things to get energy. (B24)

convection (kuhn VEHK shuhn) The transfer of thermal energy by the movement of fluids. (F33)

core (kawr) The innermost layer of Earth. (C7)

crust (kruhst) The outermost layer of Earth. (C6)

D

decay (dih KAY) To break down into simpler materials. (B48)

decomposer (dee kuhm POH zur) An organism that breaks down the remains of dead organisms. (B48)

density (DEHN sih tee) The amount of matter in a given space, or a given volume. (E25)

deposition (dehp uh ZIHSH uhn) The dropping of sediment moved by water, wind, and ice. (C29)

digestive system (dy JEHS tihv SIHS tuhm) One of the body's major organ systems. It processes the food the body takes in. (A33)

dissolve (dih ZAHLV) To mix completely with another substance to form a solution. (E58)

E

ecosystem (EE koh SIHS tuhm) All living and nonliving things that exist and interact in one place. (B6)

egg (ehg) The first stage in the life cycle of most animals. (A70)

electric cell (ih LEHK trihk sehl) A device that turns chemical energy into electrical energy. (F58)

electric charges (ih LEHK trihk CHAHRJ ehs) Tiny particles that carry units of electricity. (F44)

electric circuit (ih LEHK trihk SUR kiht) The pathway that an electric current follows. (F56)

electric current (ih LEHK trihk KUR uhnt) A continuous flow of electric charges. (F54)

electromagnet (ih lehk troh MAG niht) A strong temporary magnet that uses electricity to produce magnetism. (F68)

embryo (EHM bree oh) A plant or animal in the earliest stages of development. (A65)

energy (EHN ur jee) The ability to cause change. (E40)

environment (ehn VY ruhn muhnt) Everything that surrounds and affects a living thing. (A90, B12)

era (IHR uh) A major division of geologic time defined by events that took place during that time. (B79)

erosion (ih ROH zhuhn) The movement of rock material from one place to another. (C28)

esophagus (ih SOHF uh guhs) A muscular tube in the body that pushes food toward the stomach. (A35)

evaporation (ih vap uh RAY shuhn) The change of state from a liquid to a gas. (C42, D15)

experiment (ihks SPEHR uh muhnt) To investigate and collect data that either supports a hypothesis or shows that it is false while controlling variables and changing only one part of an experimental setup at a time.

external stimulus (ihk STUR nuhl STIHM yuh luhs) Anything in an organism's environment that causes it to react. (A94)

extinct (ihk STIHNGKT) No longer living. When the last member of a species has died, the species is extinct. (B70)

F

food chain (food chayn) The path of food energy in an ecosystem as one living thing eats another. (B38)

food web (food wehb) Two or more food chains that overlap. (B40)

force (fawrs) A push that moves an object away or a pull that moves an object nearer. (F90)

fossil (FAHS uhl) The preserved traces and remains of an organism that lived long ago. (B76)

fossil fuel (FAHS uhl FYOO uhl) A fuel that formed from the remains of ancient plants and animals. (C48)

friction (FRIHK shuhn) A force that slows or stops motion between two surfaces that are touching. (F92)

front (fruhnt) The place where two air masses meet. (D26)

G

galaxy (GAL uhk see) A huge system, or group, of stars held together by gravity. (D79)

gas giants (gas JY hunts) The four largest planets in Earth's solar system—Jupiter, Saturn, Uranus, and Neptune—that consist mainly of gases. (D57)

generator (JEHN uh ray tuhr) A devise that uses magnetism to convert energy of motion into electrical energy. (F71)

germinate (JUHR muh nayt) The process in which a seed begins to grow into a new plant. (A65)

gravity (GRAV ih tee) The force that pulls bodies or objects toward other bodies or objects. (D52, F94)

greenhouse effect (GREEN hows ih FEHKT) The process by which heat from the Sun builds up near Earth's surface and is trapped there by the atmosphere. (D10)

habitat (HAB ih tat) The place where an organism lives. (B60)

heart (hahrt) A muscular pump inside the body that pushes the blood through the blood vessels. (A42)

heat (heet) 1. The flow of thermal energy from a warmer area to a cooler area; 2. a measure of how much thermal energy is transferred from one substance to another. (E45, F32)

herbivore (HUR buh vawr) An animal that eats only plants. (B38)

hibernate (HY bur nayt) To go into a deep sleep during which an animal uses very little energy and usually does not need to eat. (B64)

humus (HYOO muhs) A material made up of decayed plant and animal matter. (C52)

hypothesize (hy PAHTH uh syz) To make an educated guess about why something happens.

igneous rock (IHG nee uhs rahk) The type of rock that is formed when melted rock from inside Earth cools and hardens. (C8)

inclined plane (ihn KLYND playn) A simple machine made up of a slanted surface. (F100)

infer (ihn FUR) To use facts and data you know and observations you have made to draw a conclusion about a specific event based on observations and data. To construct a reasonable explanation.

inherit (ihn HEHR iht) To receive traits from parents. (A79)

inherited behavior (ihn HEHR iht uhd bih HAYV yur) A behavior that an organism is born with and does not need to learn. (A100)

instinct (IHN stihngkt) A complex pattern of behavior that organisms of the same type are born with. (A101)

insulators (IHN suh lay tuhrz) Materials that electric charges do not flow through easily. (F55)

internal stimulus (ihn TUR nuhl STIHM yuh luhs) Anything within an organism that causes it to react. (A94)

kinetic energy (kuh NEHT ihk EHN ur jee) The energy that an object has because it is moving. (F7)

L

large intestine (lahrj ihn TEHS tihn) The organ where water and minerals from food are removed and absorbed into the blood. (A36)

larva (LAHR vuh) The wormlike form that hatches from an egg. The second stage of an organism that goes through complete metamorphosis. (A71)

lava (LAH vuh) Molten rock that reaches Earth's surface, such as when a volcano erupts. (C16)

leaf (leef) The part of a plant that uses sunlight and air to help the plant make food. (A18)

learned behavior (lurnd bih HAYV yur) A behavior that is taught or learned from experience. (A102)

lever (LEHV ur) A simple machine made up of a stiff bar that moves freely around a fixed point. (F102)

life cycle (lyf SY kuhl) A series of stages that occur during the lifetimes of all organisms. (A64)

life process (lyf PRAHS ehs) A function that an organism performs to stay alive and produce more of its own kind. (A6)

life span (lyf span) The length of time it takes for an individual organism to complete its life cycle. (A66)

light (lyt) A form of energy that travels in waves and can be seen when it interacts with matter. (F12)

lunar eclipse (LOO nur ih KLIHPS) An event in which the Moon passes into Earth's shadow. (D71)

M

magma (MAG muh) Molten rock beneath Earth's surface. (C16)

magnet (MAG niht) An object that attracts certain metals, mainly iron. (F62)

magnetic field (MAG neht ihk feeld) The space in which the force of a magnet can act. (F63)

magnetic poles (mag NEHT ihk pohlz) The two areas on a magnet with the greatest magnetic force. (F63)

mantle (MAN tl) A thick layer of rock between Earth's crust and core. (C7)

mass (mas) The amount of matter in an object. (E16)

matter (MAT ur) Anything that has mass and takes up space. (E6)

measure (MEHZH uhr) To use a variety of measuring instruments and tools to find the length, distance, volume, mass, or temperature using appropriate units of measurement.

metamorphic rock (meht uh MAWR fihk rahk) New rock that forms when existing rocks are changed by heat, pressure, or chemicals. (C9)

metamorphosis (meht uh MAWR fuh sihs) The process in which some organisms change form in different stages of their life cycles. (A71)

metric system (MEHT rihk SIHS tuhm) A system of measurement based on multiples of 10. (E14)

microorganism (my kroh AWR guh nihz uhm) A tiny living thing that can only be seen with a microscope. (B49)

migrate (MY grayt) To move to another region when seasons change and food supplies become scarce. (B70)

mimicry (MIHM ih kree) An adaptation that allows an animal to protect itself by looking like another kind of animal or like a plant. (B63)

mineral (MIHN ur uhl) A solid, nonliving material of specific chemical makeup. (C6)

mixture (MIHKS chur) Matter made up of two or more substances or materials that are physically combined. (E54)

molecule (MAHL ih kyool) A single particle of matter made up of two or more atoms joined together. (E7)

motion (MOH shuhn) A change in an object's position as compared to objects around it. (F82)

motor (MOH tur) A device that changes electrical energy into energy of motion. (F70)

muscular system (MUHS kyuh luhr SIHS tuhm) A system made up of muscles, tissues that make body parts move. (A54)

natural resource (NACH ur uhl REE sawrs) A material on Earth that is useful to people. (C40)

niche (nihch) The role a plant or animal plays in its habitat. (B60)

nonrenewable resource (nahn rih NOO uh buhl REE sawrs) A natural resource that cannot be replaced once it is used up or that takes thousands of years to be replaced. (C40)

nymph (nihmf) The second stage of an insect as it goes through incomplete metamorphosis. (A71)

observe (UHB zuhrv) To use the senses and tools to gather or collect information and determine the properties of objects or events.

omnivore (AHM nuh vawr) An animal that eats both plants and animals. (B38)

orbit (AWR biht) The path that Earth and eight other planets make as they move around the Sun. (D50)

organ (AWR guhn) A special part of an organism's body that performs a specific function. (A11)

organism (AWR guh nihz uhm) Any living thing that can carry out life processes on its own. (A10)

organic matter (awr GAN ihk MAT ur) The remains of plants and animals. (B6)

organ system (AWR guhn SIHS tuhm) A group of organs that work together to carry out life processes. (A12)

paleontologist (pay lee ahn TAHL uh jihst) A scientist who studies fossils. (B77)

parallel circuit (PAR uh lehl SUR kiht) A circuit in which the parts are connected so that the electric current passes along more than one pathway. (F57)

phases of the Moon (FAYZ ihz uhv thuh moon) Changes in the amount of the sunlit half of the Moon that can be seen from Earth. (D71)

photosynthesis (foh toh SIHN thih sihs) The process plants use to make food. (B36, A22)

physical change (FIHZ ih kuhl chaynj) A change in the size, shape, or state of matter that does not change it into a new kind of matter. (E38)

physical property (FIHZ ih kuhl PRAP ur tee) A characteristic of matter that can be measured or observed without changing matter into something new. (E10)

planet (PLAN iht) A large body of rock or gas that does not produce its own light and orbits around a star. (D50)

polar climate (POH lur KLY muht) Places with polar climate have very cold temperatures throughout the year, and are located around the North Pole and the South Pole. (D35)

pollinator (PAHL uh nay tur) An animal, such as an insect or bird, that helps plants make seeds by moving pollen from one part of the plant to another. (B26)

pollutant (puh LOOT uhnt) Any harmful material added to the air, the water, and the soil. (C60)

pollution (puh LOO shuhn) The addition of harmful materials to the air, the water, and the soil. (C51)

population (pahp yuh LAY shun) All the organisms of the same kind that live in an ecosystem. (B12)

position (puh ZIHSH uhn) An object's location, or place. (F82)

potential energy (puh TEHN shuhl EHN ur jee) The energy that is stored in an object. (F7)

prairie (PRAIR ee) A grassy land area with few or no trees. (B14)

precipitation (prih sihp ih TAY shuhn) Any form of water that falls from clouds to Earth's surface. (C42, D16)

predator (PREHD uh tawr) An animal that hunts other animals for food. (B37)

predict (prih DIHKT) To state what you think will happen based on past experience, observations, patterns, and cause-and-effect relationships.

prey (pray) An animal that is hunted for food by a predator. (B37)

producer (pruh DOO sur) Any organism that makes its own food. (B24)

product (PRAHD uhkt) The newly formed matter in a chemical reaction. (E67)

pulley (PUL ee) A simple machine made up of a rope fitted around the rim of a fixed wheel. (F103)

radiation (ray dee AY shuhn) The transfer of energy by waves. (F34)

rainforest (RAYN fawr ihst) An area with a great deal of rainfall. Most rainforests are warm all year, and there is a lot of sunlight. (B14)

reactant (ree AK tuhnt) The matter that you start with in a chemical reaction. (E67)

record data (rih KAWRD DAY tuh) To write (in tables, charts, journals), draw, audio record, video record, or photograph, to show observations.

recycling (ree SY kuhl ihng) The process of breaking down materials into a different form that is used again. (B48)

reflection (rih FLEHK shuhn) What occurs when light waves bounce off a surface. (F14)

refraction (rih FRAK shuhn) What occurs when light waves bend as they pass from one material to another. (F14)

renewable resource (rih NOO uh buhl REE sawrs) A natural resource that can be replaced or can replace or renew itself. (C40)

reproduce (ree pruh DOOS) When organisms make more organisms of their own kind. (A6)

reproduction (ree pruh DUHK shun) The process of making more of one's own kind. (B26)

research (rih SURCH) To learn more about a subject by looking in books, newspapers, magazines, CD-ROMs, searching the Internet, or asking science experts.

respiratory system (REHS puhr uh tawr ee SIHS tuhm) A group of organs that work together to take air into the body and push it back out. (A40)

response (rih SPAHNS) A reaction to a stimulus. (A91)

revolution (rehv uh LOO shuhn) The movement in a path around an object, as when the Earth travels around the Sun; one complete trip around the Sun. (D72)

rock (rahk) A solid material that is made up of one or more minerals. (C6)

rock cycle (rahk SY kuhl) The continuous series of changes that rocks go through. (C10)

root (root) The part of a plant that takes in water and nutrients from the ground. (A18)

rotation (roh TAY shuhn) The turning of a planet on its axis. (D68)

scavenger (SKAV uhn jur) An animal that feeds on the remains of dead animals. (B46)

screw (skroo) A simple machine made up of an inclined plane wrapped around a column. (F101)

sediment (SEHD uh muhnt) Sand, particles of rock, bits of soil, and the remains of once-living things. (C8)

sedimentary rock (sehd uh MEHN tuh ree rahk) A type of rock that forms when sediment becomes pressed together and hardens. (C8)

seed (seed) An undeveloped plant sealed in a protective coating. (A19)

seed dispersal (seed dih SPUR suhl) The scattering or carrying away of seeds from the plant that produced them. (B26)

series circuit (SIHR eez SUR kiht) A circuit in which the parts are connected so that the electric current passes through each part along a single pathway. (F57)

simple machine (SIHM puhl muh SHEEN) A device that changes a force. (F100)

skeletal system (SKEHL ih tuhl SIHS tuhm) The bones that give the body shape and support, protect the organs inside the body, and work with the muscles to move the body. (A52)

small intestine (smawl ihn TEHS tihn) The long, coiled organ where most digestion takes place. (A36)

soil (soyl) The loose material that covers much of Earth's surface. (B6)

soil profile (soyl PROH fyl) A lengthwise cross section of soil that shows the different layers. (C52)

solar system (SOH lur SIHS tuhm) A system made up of the Sun, eight planets, and smaller bodies that orbit the Sun. (D50)

solution (suh LOO shuhn) A mixture in which the particles of one kind of matter are mixed evenly with the particles of other kinds of matter. (E58)

sound (sownd) A form of energy that is produced by vibrations and can be heard. (F20)

species (SPEE sheez) A group of organisms that produces organisms of the same kind. (B70)

speed (speed) A measure of the distance an object travels in a certain amount of time. (F84)

star (stahr) A huge ball of very hot gases that gives off light, heat, and other kinds of energy. (D76)

states of matter (stayts uhv MAT ur) The three forms that matter usually takes: solid, liquid, and gas. (E8)

static electricity (STAT ihk ih lehk TRIHS ih tee) An electric charge that builds up on a material. (F46)

stem (stehm) The part of the plant that carries food, water and nutrients to and from the roots and leaves. (A18)

stimulus (STIHM yuh luhs) Anything that causes a living thing to react. (A91)

stomach (STUHM uhk) A muscular organ in the body that mixes and stores food and turns in into a soupy mix. (A35)

T

temperate climate (TEHM pur iht KLY muht) Places with temperate climate usually have warm, dry summers and cold, wet winters. (D35)

temperate zone (TEHM pur iht zohn) An area of Earth where the temperature rarely gets very hot or very cold. The temperate zones are located between the tropical zone and the polar zones. (B15)

temperature (TEHM pur uh chur)
1. A measure of how hot or cold matter is;
2. the average kinetic energy of the particles of a substance. (E46, F31)

thermal energy (THUR muhl EHN ur jee) The total kinetic energy of tiny moving particles of matter. (E44, F30)

tissue (TIHSH oo) A group of similar cells that work together. (A12)

topsoil (TAHP soyl) The upper layer of soil that contains minerals and humus. (C52)

trait (trayt) A feature or characteristic of a living thing. (A79)

tropical climate (TRAHP ih kuhl KLY miht) Places with tropical climate are hot and rainy for most of or all of the year. (D35)

universe (YOO nuh vurs) The system made up of all the matter and energy there is, including the galaxies, and their stars, planets, and moons. (D79)

use models (yooz MAHD lz) To use sketches, diagrams or other physical representation of an object, process, or idea to better understand or describe how it works.

use numbers (yooz NUHM burz) To use numerical data to count, measure, estimate, order, and record data to compare objects and events.

use variables (yooz VAIR ee uh buhlz) To keep all conditions in an experiment the same except for the variable, or the condition that is being tested in the experiment.

vein (vayn) Any blood vessel that carries blood back to the heart. (A42)

velocity (vuh LAHS ih tee) A measure of speed in a certain direction. (F86)

vibration (vy BRAY shuhn) A back-and-forth movement of matter. (F20)

volume (VAHL yoom) 1. The amount of space that matter takes up; 2. The loudness of a sound. (E17, F22)

W

water cycle (WAH tur SY kuhl) The movement of water into the air as water vapor and back to Earth's surface as precipitation. (D16)

weather (WEHTH ur) The conditions of the atmosphere at a certain place and time. (D9)

weathering (WEHTH ur ihng) The slow wearing away of rock into smaller pieces. (C26)

wedge (wehj) A simple machine made up of two inclined planes. (F101)

weight (wayt) The measure of the pull of gravity on an object. (E18)

wheel and axle (hweel and AK suhl) A simple machine made up of two cylinders that turn on the same axis. (F102)

Index

A

Acid, A35
Acid rain, C27
Adaptations, B60–B64
Adirondack Mountains, C30
Air
    composition of, D6–D7
    in forest ecosystem, B7
    and mixtures, E57
    as natural resource, C40
Air masses, D25–D26, D37
Air pollution, C51
Air pressure, D8, D22–D23
Air resistance, F92
Air sacs, A40, A41
Airplanes, F106–F107
Algae, A10
Alligators, A70, A72
Aloe vera, C41
Alps, mountains, D37
Altitude, D37
Amphibians, A70
Amplitude, F12, F22
Anemometer, D23
Angelfish, A52
Animals
    adaptations of, B60–B64
    behavior of, A100–A103,
      B64
    bones of, A52
    cells of, A8–A9
    life cycle of, A70–A72
    life span of, A72
    and reaction to
      surroundings,
      A91–A94
    as renewable resources,
      C41
    response to stimuli,
      A90–A94

Antacids, E69
Antarctica, D30–D31, D38
Anthracite, coal, C49
Ants, B22
Arctic fox, B62
Armstrong, Neil, D65
Arteries, A42–A43
Aspirin, C41
Astrolabe, D64
Astronomers, D64
Aswan Dam, B69
Atmosphere, D6–D10, D38
Atoms
    changes in, E67, E69, E71
    and molecules, E7–E9
Atriums, heart, A44
Auroras, D82
Axis
    of Earth, D68, D72
    of Moon, D71
    of planets, D72
Aye aye, B61

Bacteria, A10, B48, B49
Baking soda, E65, E69
Balance scale, E16
Ball bearings, F93
Balloons
    changes in, E1, E39,
      E46, E80
    and static electricity, F45
Barometer, D23
Bats, A1, A92, A112, B77
Battery, E68, F57, F58
Bean plants, A66
Bears, A72, A78, A102
Beavers, B13
Bedrock, C52
Bees, A92
Beetles, A24–A25, A71,
    B46, B52–B53
Bell, Alexander Graham,
    F26–F27
Bengal tigers, B62

Big Dipper, D78
Biodegradable materials,
    C62, E30–E31
Birds, A70, A72, A79
Bison, B70
Bituminous coal, C49
Blizzards, D28
Blood, A36, A40–A43
Blood circulation, A46–A49
Blood clots, A43
Blood vessels, A42–A43
Blue whale, F36–F37
Boiling, E48, E49
Bones, A52–A53
Breastbone, A53
Breathing, A40, A41
Bubbles, E56
Bumble bees, B63
Burning, E27, E28, E66, E68
Butterflies, B63

C

Cactuses, A21
Camouflage, B62
Cancer drug, E20–E21
Capillaries, A42–A43
Carbohydrates, A33–A34,
    A36
Carbon, B79
Carbon dioxide, A22,
    A40–A41, B36, D7
Cardiac muscle, A54
Caribou, B70
Carnivores, B38–B39,
    B47, B48
Carrion beetles, A24, B46
Carson, Rachel, B42–B43
Cartilage, A53
Cassini **spacecraft,** D59
Cell membrane, A8–A9
Cell wall, A8
Cells, A8–A9
Celsius scale, E46–E47
Cenozoic Era, B79
Centimeters, E14–E15, E17

Chemical bonds, E69, E70
Chemical changes, E66–E71
Chemical combination, E71
Chemical compound, E71
Chemical energy, F8
Chemical properties,
    E27–E28
Chemical reaction, E67–E69
Chimpanzees, A102
Chlorophyll, A8, A22
Chloroplasts, A8, A22
Chromosomes, A8–A9
Circuit box, F58
Circuit breaker, F58
Circuit pathways, F57
Circulatory system,
    A42–A44, A46–A49
Cirrus clouds, D17
Clay soil, C53
Climate, D34–D38
Climate zones, D35
Clouds, C42, D16–D17,
    F48–F51
Clown fish, B23
Coal,
    coke from, C49
    formation of, C49
    as fossil fuel, C48
Color
    and light, F15–F16
    of matter, E6, E24, E50
Comets, D62
Community, B12
Compass, F64
Compost, B50
Condensation
    and clouds, D16–D17
    as physical change, E48,
        E49
    and water cycle,
        D16–D17, D49
    and water vapor, C39,
        C42
Conduction, F32
Conductors, F55, F57, F70
Conservation, B72–B73,
    C60–C63

Constellations, D78
Consumers, B24–B25, B36,
    B37, B46
Continents, C6
Convection, F33
Cooking, E28, E66–E67, F32
Copper, E70
Coral reef ecosystem, B1,
    B16, B88
Core, of Earth, C7
Crabs, A82–A83, B25
Crafty Canines, B19
Crayfish, A92
Crickets, A92
Crocodile, B23
Crust, of Earth, C6, C8–C9,
    C15
Crystals, C8
Cubic centimeters, E17
Cumulonimbus clouds, D17
Cumulus clouds, D17
Cylinders, E17
Cytoplasm, A8–A9, A11

Day and night, D68–D69
Decay, B48–B50
Decibels, F36–F37
Decomposers, B48–B50
Deer, B13, B39, B62
Deinotherium, fossil, B78
Density, E25, E50, E55
Deposition, C29
    see also Erosion
Desert, D37
Desert ecosystem, B8, B61
Diaphragm, A40–A41
Diatoms, A10
Digestion, A34–A36
Digestive system, A12,
    A32–A36
Dinosaurs, B76, B79
Direction, and motion, F86
Disease, A10, B48
Distance, measuring,
    F84–F85

Dogs, A94, A103
Dolphins, A92, B60
Douglas, Marjory
    Stoneman, B72
Ducks, A6, B60
Dung beetles, B52–B53

E

E. coli, A10
Eagles, B73
Eardrum, F24
Ears, A90, F24
Earth
    atmosphere of, D6–D10,
        D38
    axis of, D68, D72
    core of, C7
    crust of, C6–C7, C8–C9,
        C15
    diameter of, D48, D51,
        D57
    gravity of, D52
    layers of, C6–C7
    as magnet, F64
    mantle of, C7, C16
    mass of, D51, D57
    and Moon, D57,
        D70–D71
    orbit of, D50–D51,
        D68–D69
    revolution of, D72
    rotation of, D68–D69,
        D72, D78
    and Sun, D48–D49, D56
    surface of, C26–C30, D51
    warming of, D38,
        D48–D49
    water on, C42–C43, D14
Earth Day, B73
Earthquakes, C14–C15, C18
Echolocation, A92, A112
Eclipse, of Moon, D71
Ecosystems
    and living things,
        B12–B16

and nonliving things,
B6–B8
relationships in, B24–B25
types of, B7–B8,
B12–B16, B37–B39
see also Environment

Eggs
of amphibians, A70
of animals, A70
of birds, A70, A72
of fish, A70
of insects, A70, A71
and life cycle, A70–A71
of reptiles, A70

Egyptian plover, B23

El Niño, D36

Electric cell, F58

Electric charges, F44–F46,
F54–F55

Electric circuit, F56–F58

Electric cord, F54–F55

Electric current, F54–F58,
F71

Electric eel, F74–F75

Electric fuses, F58

Electric motor, F70

Electric outlet, F54

Electric switch, F52, F56

Electric wires, F71

Electrical appliances,
F54–F55, F58, F72

Electrical energy, F8

Electrician, F105

Electricity
cost of, F72
from fossil fuels,
C48–C51
generating, F58, F71
and magnetism, F68–F71
saving, F72

Electromagnets, F68–F70

Elephants, A72, B78

Elion, Gertrude Belle,
E20–E21

Embryo, A65, A70

Endurance, D30–D31

Energy
changes in, E40, E44–E45,
E66–E69, F7–F8
from food, B34–B40
forms of, E46–E49, F6–F8,
F12–F13, F19–F21,
F30–F33
from fossil fuels, C48–C51
from Sun, B36, C51,
D48–D49, D76

Energy transformation, F8

Environment
changes in, B68–B69
for living things, B12
protecting, C61
reacting to, A90–A94
see also Ecosystems

Environmental technicians,
D81

Enzymes, A34, A35

Equator, D25, D35, D36

Erosion, C28–C29. *See also*
Weathering *and*
Deposition.

Eruptive prominence,
D82–D83

Esophagus, A35

Evaporation, C42, D15–D16,
D49, E49

Exhaling, A40, A41

Exoskeleton, A52

External stimulus, A90, A94

Extinction, B70, B78

Eyes, A90

F

Fahrenheit scale, E46–E47

Fats, as nutrients, A33, A36

Faults, C14–C16, C30

Femur, bone, A53

Fertilizers, C44

Fiber optics, F27

Fibrous root system, A20

Fibula, bone, A53

Fir trees, A66

Fire investigator, E73

Fires, C18, E66

"First Snow," E62–E63

Fish
eggs of, A70
gills of, A40
instincts of, A101
and interdependence,
B23, B82
skeletal system of, A52
in tropical climate, D34

Five senses, A90–A91

Flight, E1, E46, E80,
F106–F107

Florida Everglades, B15,
B72

Flowers, A19, A24–A25,
A64–A65, B26

Fog, E57

Food
changes in, E66–E68
cooking, E28, E66–E67,
F32
digesting, A32–A36
see also Nutrients

Food chains, B38–B40

Food science technician,
E73

Food webs, B40

Forces, and motion,
F90–F94

Forest destruction, C61

Forest ecosystem, B6–B7,
B12–B13

Forest fires, C18

Forest food chain, B38–B39

Fossil fuels, C48–C51

Fossil tree fern, B76

Fossils, B76–B79, D38

Fox, B37, B40

Franklin, Benjamin, F48–F51

Freezing, E48–E49

Frequency, F22–F23

Friction, F86, F90–F94

Frogs, A80, B63

Index

Fuel oil, C50
Fulgurites, E74–E75
Fungi, B48, B49, B68

Galaxies, D79
Galilei, Galileo, D64
Galle, Johann, D65
Garbage, B50, C60–C61
Gas giants, D57–D61
Gases
    in atmosphere, D6–D10
    changes in, E48–E49
    mixtures of, E56
    particles of, E48–E49
    properties of, E8–E10
    water vapor, D14, E8–E9
Generator, F71
Geologic time scale, B79
Germination, A65, A66
Gills, A40
Giraffes, E14, E15
Glaciers, C28–C29
Golden Hoard, The,
    E62–E63
Goldenrod spider, B83
Goosefish, B82
Grams, E16
Grand Canyon, C20–C23
Grasshoppers, B40
Gravity
    of Earth, D52
    and friction, F86, F90–F94
    of Moon, D52
    and weight, D52, E18
Great horned owl, B38–B39
Green homes, C56–C57
Greenhouse effect, D10
Grizzly bear, A72
Grosbeak weaver birds,
    A101
Groundwater, D16
Group hunting, B64

Habitats, B60–B61
    See also Ecosystems;
    Environment
Hail, D18
Hearing, A90, A92, F24
Heart, A42, A44, A54
Heat
    from Sun, D10, D24, F13
    from thermal energy,
      E45, F30–F32
Helios, F106–F107
Herbivores, B38, B39
Hermit crabs, B25
Herschel, William, D60, D64
Hibernation, A101, B64
Himalayas, mountains, C30
Hitchings, Dr. George,
    E20–E21
Hooke, Robert, A14–A15
Hot-air balloon, E1, E46,
    E80
Human body
    circulatory system,
      A42–A44, A46–A49
    digestive system,
      A32–A36
    muscular system, A54
    respiratory system,
      A40–A41, A46–A49
    skeletal system, A52–A53
Humans
    inheriting traits, A79
    life span of, A72
    traits in, A79
Humerus, bone, A53
Humidity, D22, D25
Humpback whales, B64
Humus, C52, C53
Hurricanes, D22, D28
Hydroelectric power, C51
Hypatia, D64

Ice
    freezing, D14
    melting, D15, E39–E40,
      E48–E50
    as solid, E8–E9
    and weathering, C27
Igneous rock, C8–C10
In-line skates, F96–F97
Inclined plane, F100
Infrared camera, E47
Inhaling, A40, A41
Inheriting behavior, A100
Inheriting traits, A78–A80
Insects
    eggs of, A70, A71
    inheriting traits, A79
    instincts of, A101
    as pollinators, B26
Instinct, A101
Insulators, F55
Internal stimulus, A94
Intestines, A36
Iron, E44–E45, E50
Iron filings, E54, F63

Jackrabbit, B61
Jellies, A11
Joints, A53
Jupiter, D57, D58, D72

Kapok tree, B24
Kilograms, E16
Kilometers, E14–E15
Kinetic energy, F6–F8,
    F30–F31
Kingfisher, A94

L

Landfills, C60
Landforms, C15
Landscaper, B81
Landslides, C18
Large intestine, A36
Larva, A71
Latitude, D36
Lava, C16–C17, C32–C33
Leaf-cutter ants, B68
Leafy sea dragon, B63
Learned behavior,
    A102–A103
Leaves
    and photosynthesis, A22,
       B36, D49
    role of, A18–A20, A22
    types of, A20
Lemur, A79
Lever, F102
Licensed practical nurse,
    A105
Life cycles
    of animals, A70–A72
    of plants, A64–A65
Life processes, A6–A7,
    A16–A22
Life span
    of animals, A72
    of plants, A66
Ligaments, A53
Light
    absorption of, F15
    behavior of, F12–F16
    and color, F15–F16
    in forest ecosystem, B7
    properties of, F12–F13
    reflection of, D50,
       D70–D71, F14
    speed of, F85
    from Sun, D76, F13
Light bulbs, F56, F57
Light energy, F8, F12–F13

Light switch, F56
Light waves, F12–F15,
    F26–F27
Lightning, D40–D41,
    E74–E75, F48–F51
Lightning fossils, E74–E75
Lignite, coal, C49
Liquids
    changes in, E48–E49
    measuring, E17
    mixtures of, E56
    particles of, E44–E45,
       E48–E49
    properties of, E8–E10
    volume of, E17
Liters, E17
Liver, A36
Living things
    adaptations of, B60–B64
    characteristics of, A6–A12,
       A78–A80
    community of, B12
    and ecosystems, B12–B16
    inheriting traits, A78–A80
    and interdependence,
       B22–B23
    and reproduction, A6–A7,
       A64–A65, A70–A72,
       B26
    roles of, B22–B26
    see also Organisms
Lizards, A12, A72
Loam, C53
Lunar eclipse, D71
Lungs, A40–A41

 M

Macaws, B24
Magma, C16–C17
Magnetic compass, F64
Magnetic field, F63, F64
Magnetic poles, F63, F64,
    F70
Magnetism, F62, F68–F71

Magnets, F62–F63
Mammals, A72. *See also*
    Animals
Manatees, B28–B29
Mantle, of Earth, C7, C16
Many-celled organisms,
    A11
Maple trees, A66
Marabou storks, B47
Mars, D56, D57, D65, D72
Mars rovers, D65
Mass, E14–E16, E50
Materials
    biodegradable materials,
       C62, E30–E31
    recycling materials, C58,
       C62–C63
    reusing materials,
       C62–C63
Matter
    chemical changes in,
       E66–E71
    classifying, E24–E25
    and energy, E40, E44–E45
    examples of, E6, E26
    makeup of, E6–E7
    mass of, E16
    measuring, E14–E19
    observing, E6–E7
    particles of, E7–E8,
       E44–E49
    physical changes in, E10,
       E38–E40, E44–E49,
       E70–E71
    properties of, E6–E8,
       E24–E27, E50
    states of, E8, E10, E48–E49
    volume of, E17
Mealworms, A71
Mechanical energy, F8
Melting, D15, E39–E40,
    E48–E50, E74–E75
Mercury, D56, D57, D72
Merlin, Joseph, F96
Mesosphere, D9

Index

Mesozoic Era, B79

Metals, E27–E28, E50, E68, E70

Metamorphic rock, C9–C10

Metamorphosis, A71

Meteorologists, D27, D28, D81

Meters, E14–E15

Metric ruler, E14–E15

Metric system, E14–E15

Metric units, E15, E17

Mexican bean beetle, A71

Micrographia, A14–A15

Microorganisms, B49

Microscopes, A14, E6–E7

Midnight Fox, The, B18

Migration, A101, B70

Milky Way Galaxy, D79

Milliliters, E17

Mimicry, B63

Minerals
   digestion of, A36
   as nutrients, A33
   rocks, C6, C8
   in soil, C52

Mist, D15

Mites, C66–C67

Mitochondria, A8–A9

Mixtures, E54–E60, E71

Moeritherium, B78

Mold, B48

Molecules
   and atoms, E7–E9
   changes in, E67, E69, E71

Moles, A91

Molten rock, C10, C16

Monkeys, A103, B25

Moon
   axis of, D71
   diameter of, D51
   and Earth, D57, D68–D71
   eclipse of, D71
   gravity of, D52
   and light, D50, D70–D71
   mass of, D51
   orbit of, D70–D71

   phases of, D70–D71
   rotation of, D71
   surface of, D51
   walking on, D65

Moths, A92

Motion, F82–F85, F90–F94

Motors, F70

Mount Paricutín, C30

Mount St. Helens, C16–C18

Mountain lion, A72

Mountains, C15–C17, C30, D37

Mouse, A72

Mudslides, C18

Muir, John, B72, B73

Muscles, A54, A56–A57

Muscular system, A54

Mushrooms, B48

Musical instruments, F21, F22

Musk ox, B61

National Park Service, B72

Natural gas, C50

Natural resources, C48–C54, C60–C63

Nectar, B26

Neptune, D57, D61, D65, D72

Niche, B60

Night vision goggles, A96–A97

Nile River, B69

Nitrogen, D6–D7

Nonliving things, B6–B8

Nonrenewable resources, C40, C48–C54

North Pole, D25, F64

Nose, A41, A90

Nucleus, A8–A9

Nutrients
   in blood, A36, A42–A43
   in food, A33

   energy from, A32
   and life processes, A6–A7
   in soil, B48–B50, C44, C52
   types of, A33
   see also Food

Nymph, A71

Oceans
   currents of, D36
   and deposition, C29
   ecosystems in, B16
   as habitat, B60
   interdependence in, B23
   warming of, D24, D36, D48
   and water cycle, D16
   and weathering, C26

Offspring, A71, A78–A80

Oil, C50–C51

Olsen, Brennan, F96

Olsen, Scott, F96

Omnivores, B38, B39, B47

Opossum, B60

Opportunity, Mars rover, D65

Orb spiders, A101

Orbit, D50–D51, D68–D71

Orca whale, A102

Orchard Book of Greek Myths, The, A74

Organ system,
   circulatory system, A42–A44, A46–A49
   digestive system, A32–A36
   muscular system, A54
   organization of, A11–A12
   respiratory system, A40–A41, A46–A49
   skeletal system, A52–A53

Organic matter, B6

Organisms
   adaptations of, B60–B64

inheriting traits, A78–A80

response to stimuli, A90–A94

types of, A10–A12

see also Living things

Otters, A93, A102

Owl butterfly, B63

Owls, B38–B40

Oxygen

in blood, A46–A49

need for, D6–D7

from plants, A10, A22

Pacific yew trees, A66

Paleontologist, B77–B79

Paleozoic Era, B79

Palm tree, A79

Pancreas, A36

Pandas, B66

Parallel circuit, F57–F58

Park ranger, B81

Parkes Radio Telescope, D65

Particles

and chemical changes, E67, E70

of matter, E7–E8, E44–E49

movement of, E44–E49, F30–F33

observing, E6–E7

and physical changes, E44–E49

Passenger pigeons, B70

Pathologist, A105

Peat, C49

Peccaries, B47

Pelvis, bone, A53

Petals, A64, A65

Phiomia, B78

Photosynthesis, A22, B36, B38, D49

Physical changes, of matter, E10, E38–E40, E44–E50, E70–E71

Physical combination, E71

Physical properties, of matter, E10, E24–E26

Pigeons, Passenger, B70

Pistil, A64, A65

Pitch, F23

Planets, D50–D51, D56–D62, D72

Plant cells, A8

Plants

adaptation of, B60–B61

classifying, A20–A21

energy from, B37–B38

in food chain, B38–B39, B40

inheriting traits, A79–A80

life cycle of, A64–A65

life span of, A66

nutrients for, C44

parts of, A18–A21

as producers, B24

as renewable resources, C41

reproduction of, A64–A65, B26

response to stimuli, A91, A94

and sunlight, D49

see also Trees

Platelets, A43

Plimpton, James, F96

Pluto, D57, D62

Poison dart frog, B63

Polar air masses, D25

Polar bears, A78

Polar climate, D35

Polar ecosystem, B8

Poles, D25, D38, F63–F64, F70

Pollen, A64–A65, B26

Pollination, A64–A65, B26

Pollinators, B26

Pollutants, C60

Pollution, C51, C60

Pond ecosystem, B37, B39

Pond food chain, B39

Ponderosa pine trees, A66

Populations, B12

Position, and motion, F82–F83

Potential energy, F6–F8

Powell, John Wesley, C20–C23

Powell Expedition, C20–C23

Prairie ecosystem, B14

Praying mantis, B83

Precipitation, C42, D16, D18, D23

Predators, B37, B39, B47, B62–B64

Prey, B37, B39, B46–B47, B63–B64

Prism, F16

Producers, B24, B37, B38

Protection, B22, B25

Proteins, A32–A33, A35–A36

Pterosaur, B77

Pull, F90–F91, F94

Pulley, F103

Pulse, A44

Pupa, A71

Push, F90–F91

Pygmy seahorse, B83

Rabbits, A91, B25, B37, B64

Raccoons, A102, B39, B40

Radiant energy, F13

Radiation, F13, F34

Radio waves, F26

Radius, bone, A53

Rain, D12, D18, D22–D23, D49

Rain gauge, D23

Rainbow, F16
Rainforests
    destruction of, C61
    ecosystems, B14, B24–B25
    flowers in, A24–A25
    as habitat, B60, B61
Ramps, F100
Rats, A102
Reactants, E67, E69, E70
Reaction to surroundings,
    A7, A90–A94
Recycling materials,
    C62–C63
Recycling matter, B46–B50
Red blood cells, A43, A48
Redwood trees, A66
Reflection, of light, F14
Reflex, A100
Refraction, of light, F14
Reis, Johann, F26
Renewable resources,
    C40–C44
Reproduction
    of animals, A70–A72
    as a life process, A6–A7,
      A72
    of living things, A6–A7,
      A64–A65, A70–A72,
      B26
    of plants, A64–A65, B26
    see also Life cycles
Reptiles, A70
Respiratory system,
    A40–A41, A46–A49
Reusing materials, C62–C63
Revolution, of planets, D72
Rezazadeh, Hossein, A56
Rhinoceros beetle, A56–A57
Ribs, bones, A52, A53
Robotics engineer, F105
Rock cycle, C10, C54
Rocks
    and erosion, C28
    formation of, C6–C7, C54
    layers of, C20–C23
    in soil, C52

    types of, C8–C9
    and weathering, C8, C10,
      C26–C29
Roller coasters, F1, F112
Roller skates, F96–F97
Root systems, A20
Roots, A18–A20, A22, C27
Rotation
    of Earth, D68–D69, D72,
      D78
    of Moon, D71
    of planets, D72
Rusting metal, E27–E28,
    E68

S

Saber-toothed tigers, B79,
    D38
Saliva, A34
Salt water, E58–E60
Sand
    melting, E74–E75
    mixtures of, E54, E58,
      E60
    and soil, C53
    solubility of, E60
Saturn, D57, D59, D65, D72
Scarlet macaws, B24
Scavengers, B46–B48
Screw, F101
Sea anemone, B23
Sea breeze, D24
Sea otters, A93, A102
Sea stacks, C26–C27
Sea slug, B62
Sea stars, A79, A80
Sea turtles, A100
Sea water, E58–E59
Seahorse, B83
Seals, A80, D34
Seasons, D68–D69
Secret World of Spiders,
    The, A75
Sediment, C8, C29

Sedimentary rock, C8–C10
Seed dispersal, B26
Seeds
    from flowers, A19,
      A64–A65, B26
    from fruits, B26
    germinating, A65
    planting, A66
    scattering, B26
    sprouting, A64
Seeing, A90
Seismologist, C65
Sense organs, A90–A93
Series circuit, F57
Severe weather, D28
Shackleton, Sir Ernest,
    D30–D31
Shade, B7
Shadows, F13
Shape, of matter, E6, E24
Shelter, B22, B25
Sierra Club, B72
Sierra Nevada Mountains,
    C30
Silent Spring, B42–B43
Silt, C53
Simmons, Philip, E50
Simple machines,
    F100–F103
Single-celled organisms,
    A10
Skates, F96–F97
Skeletal muscle, A54
Skeletal system, A52–A53
Skin, A90
Skull, A53
Skunks, B25, B38–B39, D34
Skydiving, F94
Sleet, D18
Sloths, A96–A97
Small intestine, A36
Smelling, A90, A93
Smooth muscle, A54
Snakes, A93, B40
Snow, D18, E62–E63
Snowboard, F93

Soil
 destruction of, C61
 erosion of, C28
 in forest ecosystem, B7
 layers of, C52
 makeup of, B6
 minerals in, C52
 as natural resource, C44, C52–C53
 nutrients in, B48–B50, C44, C52
 pollution of, C60
 properties of, C52–C53
 rocks in, C52
 types of, C53
Soil horizons, C52
Soil mites, C66–C67
Soil profile, C52
Solar cells, F107
Solar energy systems installer, C65
Solar eruptions, D82–D83
Solar power, C51
Solar system, D50–D51, D56–D57, D64–D65, D79
Solids
 changes in, E48–E49
 mass of, E14–E16
 and mixtures, E56
 particles of, E44–E45, E48–E49
 properties of, E8–E10
 volume of, E17
Solubility, E60
Solutions, E58–E60
Sound, F20–F24, F36–F37
Sound energy, F8, F20–F21
Sound waves, A92, F22–F23
South Pole, D25, D38
Space probes, D65
Species, B70
Speed, and motion, F84–F85
Spiders, A75, A101, B83
Spine, A52

Spirit, Mars rover, D65
Spring scale, E18
Springs, F7, F20
Stamen, A64, A65
Starches, A34
Stars, D1, D76–D79
State, changes in, E48–E49
Static electricity, F44–F46
Steam, E8, E10
Stems, A18–A19, A21, A22
Stimuli, A90–A94
Stomach, A32, A35
Stratosphere, D9
Stratus clouds, D17
Strip mining, C48
Succulents, A20
Sugar
 as carbohydrate, A34
 chemical changes in, E70–E71
 and photosynthesis, A22, B36
 physical changes of, E70–E71
 solubility of, E60
Sun
 diameter of, D48, D51
 and Earth, D48–D49, D56
 energy from, B36, C51, D48–D49, D76
 heat from, D7, D10, D24, D48–D49, D76, F13
 light from, D76, F13
 mass of, D51
 orbiting, D50–D51, D68–D69
 and solar eruptions, D82–D83
 and solar system, D50–D51, D56–D57, D64–D65, D79
 surface of, D51
 and water cycle, D16, D49

Tadpole, A80
Tamarin monkey, B25
Tapir, B24
Taproot system, A20
Tasting, A90, A92
Telephone, F26–F27
Telescopes, D64
Temperate climate, D35
Temperate zone, B15, D35
Temperature, D23, D25, E46–E49, F30–F31
Termites, A106–A107
Terrarium, B16
Texture, of matter, E6, E25
Thermal energy
 changes in, E44–E50
 heat from, E45, F30–F32
 and matter, E44–E45
 and radiant energy, F13
 and temperature, E46–E47, F30–F31
 transfer of, F8, F32–F33
Thermometers, D23, E46–E47
Thermosphere, D9
Thorn bug, A52
Throat, A40
Thunderstorms, D26–D27, D40–D41
Tibia, bone, A53
Tissues, A12, A32, A54
Titan, moon of Saturn, D65
Titan arum, flower, A24–A25
Topsoil, C52
Tornadoes, D26, D28, D40–D41
Toucan, B60
Touching, A90
Trachea, A40, A41
Traits, A79–A80
Trash, C60–C63, E30–E31

Trees
life cycle of, A64
life span of, A66
as producers, B24
as renewable resources, C41
rings of, D38
as shelter, B25
see also Plants
Trillium plants, B12–B13
Trilobites, B79
Triton, moon of Neptune, D62
Tropical air masses, D25
Tropical climate, D35
Tropical fish, D34
Troposphere, D8–D9
Tundra habitat, B61

Ulna, bone, A53
Universe, D76, D79. *See also* Solar system
Uranus, D57, D60, D64, D72
Ursa Major, D78

Vacuoles, A8–A9
Veins, A42–A43
Velociraptor, B79
Velocity, F86
Ventricles, heart, A44
Venus, D56, D57, D72
Vertebra, bones, A53
Vibrations, F20–F21, F23
Villi, A36
Vitamins, A33
Volcanoes, C16–C18, C32–C33
Voles, B38, B40
Volume
sound, F22
spatial, E14–E15, E17

Volvox, A11
Voyager 2, D60

Warm air mass, D26, D37
Warm climates, D34–D35
Warning coloration, B63
Water
and deposition, C29
on Earth, C42, D14
and erosion, C28
in forest ecosystem, B7
as natural resource, C40, C42–C43
for plants, A22
states of, D14–D15, E8
warming of, D24, D34, D36, D48
Water cycle, C42, D16, D49
Water droplets, D17
Water vapor
and clouds, D17
and condensation, C42
and evaporation, C42, D15–D16, D49, E49
as gas, D14, E8–E9
and precipitation, D37
Watson, Thomas, F26
Wavelength, F12, F16, F22
Waves, of energy, F12–F15, F22–F23, F26–F27
Weather,
and atmosphere, D9
data, D22, D27
factors of, D22–D23
forecasts, D27, D28
fronts, D26, D27
maps, D27
patterns of, D26
Weathering, C8, C10, C26–C29
Wedge, F101
Weight, D52, E18
Whales, A101–A102, B64, F36–F37

Wheel and axle, F102
Wheels, F93, F96–F97
White blood cells, A43
Wildfires, C18
Wind
causes of, D24, D48
and deposition, C29
and erosion, C28
measuring, D23
and weather, D22
Windpipe, A41
Wind power, C51
Wind speed, D23, D41
Wood duck, B60
Woodchucks, B25
Woodpecker, B40
Woolly mammoths, B78, D38

Yellowstone National Park, B72

Zebras, B64

Credits

Permission Acknowledgments

Excerpt from *The Secret World of Spiders*, by Theresa Greenaway, illustrated by Tim Hayward and Stuart Lafford. Copyright © 2001 Steck-Vaughn Company. Reprinted by permission of Steck-Vaughn Company, an imprint of Harcourt Education International. Excerpt from "Arachne the Spider" from the *Orchard Book of Greek Myths*, retold by Geraldine McCaughrean, illustrated by Emma Chichester Clark. First published in the U.K. by Orchard Books in 1992. Text copyright © 1992 by Geraldine McCaughrean. Illustrations copyright © 1992 by Emma Chichester Clark. Reprinted by permission of The Watts Publishing Group and Margaret K. McElderry Books, an imprint of Simon & Schuster Children's Publishing Division. Excerpt from "The Alligator" from *The Florida Water Story: From Raindrops to the Sea*, by Peggy Sias Lantz and Wendy A. Hale. Copyright © 1998 by Peggy Sias Lantz and Wendy A. Hale. Reprinted by permission of Pineapple Press, Inc. Excerpt from *Animals in Danger: Florida Manatee*, by Rod Theodorou. Copyright © 2001 by Reed Educational & Professional Publishing. Reprinted by permission of Harcourt Education. Excerpt from "The Search" from *The Midnight Fox*, by Betsy Byars, illustrated by Ann Grifalconi. Copyright © 1968 by Betsy Byars. Reprinted by permission of Viking Penguin, A Division of Penguin Young Readers Group, A Member of Penguin Group (USA) Inc., 345 Hudson Street, New York, NY 10014. All rights reserved. Excerpt from *Crafty Canines: Coyotes, Foxes, and Wolves*, by Phyllis J. Perry. Copyright © 1999 by Franklin Watts. All rights reserved. Reprinted by permission of Franklin Watts, an imprint of Scholastic Library Publishing. Excerpt from "First Snow: A Native American Myth" from *The Golden Hoard: Myths and Legends of the World* by Geraldine McCaughrean, illustrated by Bee Willey. Text copyright © 1995 by Geraldine McCaughrean. Illustrations copyright © 1995 by Bee Willey. Reprinted by permission of Orion Children's Books and Margaret K. McElderry Books, an imprint of Simon & Schuster Children's Publishing Division.

Cover

(Lizard) JH Pete Carmichael/Getty Images. (Rock) Digital Vision/Getty Images. (Desert bkgd) Photodisc/Getty Images. (Back cover lizard) (Spine) © David A Northcott/CORBIS. (Cactus) © George H. H. Huey/CORBIS.

Photography

Unit A Opener: Anup Shah/Nature Picture Library. **A1** Merlin D. Tuttle/Bat Conservation International. **A2–A3** (bkgd) Darrell Gulin/DRK photo. **A3** (b) David Noton Photography/Alamy Images. (tr) Claudia Kunin/Corbis. **A4** (bl) Mattias Klum/ National Geographic/Getty Images. **A4–A5** (bkgd) Freeman Patterson/Masterfile. **A6** (b) J. David Andrews/Masterfile. (bl) GK Hart/ Vikki Hart/Photodisc/Getty Images. **A7** (tl) John Beedle/Alamy Images. (tr) David Young–Wolff/Photo Edit Inc. (cl) M. T. Frazie/ Photo Researchers, Inc. (cr) Francois Gohier/ Photo Researchers, Inc. **A7** (bl) © Dwight Kuhn Photography. (br) Gail M. Shumway/ Bruce Coleman Inc **A8** © Dwight Kuhn Photography. **A9** Carolina Biological/Visuals Unlimited/Getty Images. **A10** (l) © E.R. Degginger/Dembinsky Photo Associates. (r) S. Lowry/Univ Ulster/Stone/Getty Images. **A11** (r) © Bill Curtsinger/National Geographic/Getty Images. (l) Kim Taylor/Bruce Coleman Inc. **A12** (tl) Peter Weber/ Photograper's Choice/Getty Images. (c) William b. Rhoten. **A13** (t) GK Hart/Vikki Hart/Photodisc/Getty Images. (c) Kim Taylor/ Bruce Coleman Inc. (b) Peter Weber/ Photograper's Choice/Getty Images. **A14** (br) The Granger Collection. (tl) The Granger Collection. (Frame) Image Farm. **A15** (cr) Omikron/Photo Researchers, Inc. (t) © 1998 from the Warnock Library. Imaged by Octavo (www.octavo.com). Used with permission. **A16** (bl) Art Wolfe/The Image Bank/Getty Images. **A16–A17** (bkgd) Stephen J. Krasemann/DRK photo. **A18** Gary Braasch/Corbis. **A19** Peter Chadwick/DK Images. **A20** (tl) © E.R. Degginger/Photo Researchers, Inc. (cl) A. Pasieka/Photo Researchers, Inc. (bl) Richard Parker/Photo Researchers, Inc. (bc) Michael Boys/Corbis. (br) Michael P. Gadomski/Photo Researchers, Inc. **A21** (bl) Photri. (t) R. A. Mittermeier/ Bruce Coleman Inc. (br) Steve Gorton/DK Images. **A23** (t) Peter Chadwick/DK Images. (c) Michael Boys/Corbis. **A28–A29** (bkgd) Philippe Montigny/Vandystandt/The Image Pro Shop Ltd. **A29** (tr) Pete A. Eising/ Stockfood Munich/Stockfood America. (c) Roy Morsch/Corbis. (br) Lester Lefkowitz/ Corbis. **A30** (bl) John Burwell/Foodpix. **A30–A31** © M I (Spike) Walker/Alamy. **A35** (tl) © E.R. Degginger/Color Pic, Inc. **A38–A39** Stephen Frink/Corbis. **A40** (bl) Charles V. Angelo/Photo Researchers, Inc. **A41** Pemberton/PhoOtri Inc. **A43** (tr) P. Motta & S. Correr/Photo Researchers, Inc. **A50** (bl) Lawrence Migdale. **A50–A51** (bkgd) P. Leonard/Zefa/Masterfile. **A52** (bl)Frank Greenaway/DK Images. (r) Dave Roberts/ Science Photo Library. **A54** Steve Shott/DK Images. **A55** (b) Steve Shott/DK Images. **A60–A61** (bkgd) Michel & Christine Denis– Hout/Photo Researchers, Inc. **A61** (tr) Keith Brofsky/Getty Images. (c) Jane Sapinsky/ Superstock. (br) John Daniels/Ardea London Ltd. (bl) Dennis Flaherty/Photo Researchers, Inc. **A62–A63** (bkgd) Marc Moritsch/National Geographic Image Collection. **A68** (bl) Tom Lazar/Earth Scenes/Animals Animals. **A68–A69** (bkgd) © Peter Arnold, Inc./Alamy. **A70** (tc) Marty Cordano/DRK photo. (tr) Joe McDonald/Bruce Coleman Inc. (b) Jerry Young/DK Images **A71** (l) Alan & Linda Detrick/Photo Researchers, Inc. (t) Gilbert S. Grant/Photo Researchers, Inc. (b) Kent Wood/Photo Researchers, Inc. (r) Bill Beatty. **A73** (t) Marty Cordano/DRK Photo. (c) Gilbert S. Grant/Photo Researchers, Inc. **A75** (bkgd) Kim Taylor/Bruce Coleman Inc. **A76** (bl) Bahr/Picturequest. **A76–A77** (bkgd) Charles Krebs/Corbis. **A78** T Davis/ W Bilenduke/Getty Images. **A79** (c) W. Schroll/ Zefa/Masterfile. (t) Frans Lanting/Minden Pictures. (b) Sylvaine Achernar/The Image bank/Getty Images. **A80** (b) Dan Guravich/ Corbis. (c) Dan Suzio/Photo Researchers, Inc. (t) Breck P. Kent/ Earth Scenes/Animals Animals. **A86–A87** (bkgd) David A Northcott/Corbis. **A87** (tr) Sanford/ Agliolo/ Corbis. (c) John Eastcott & Yva Momatiuk/ Natinal Geographic Image Collection. **A88** (bl) John Daniels/Ardea. **A88–A89** (bkgd) T. Ozonas/Dembinsky Photo Associates. **A90** (bl) Michael D. L. Jordan/Dembinsky Photo Associates, Inc. **A90** (br) © E.R. Degginger/Color Pic, Inc. **A91** (tl) © blickwinkel/Alamy. (tr) © blickwinkel/ Alamy. (t) © blickwinkel/Alamy.(br) Michael Quinton/Minden Pictures. **A92** (b) Stephen Dalton/NHPA. (t) Frank Greenaway/DK Images. **A93** (t) J. Westrich/Zefa/Masterfile. (b) Stephen J. Krasemann/DRK Photo. **A94** (b) © Dwight Kuhn Photography. (t) © blickwinkel/Alamy. **A95** (t) Michael Quinton/ Minden Pictures. (c) J. Westrich/Zefa/ Masterfile. (b) © Dwight Kuhn Photography. **A96** (br) Geoff Dann/DK Images. **A96–A97** (bkgd) Gergory Dimijian/Science Photo Library/Photo Researchers, Inc. **A97** (tr) Urs Hauenstein/Photo Atlas. **A98** (bl) Steve Bloom/Alamy Images. **A98–A99** (bkgd) Adam Jones/Photo Researchers, Inc. **A100–101** (bkgd) Mike Parry/Minden Pictures. **A101** (br) Mitsuaki Iwago/Minden Pictures. (tr) Stephen J. Krasemann/DRK Photo. **A102** Jack Sullivan/Alamy Images. **A103** (cr) Lawrence Migdale. (b) Herbert Kehrer/ Photo Researchers, Inc. **A105** (tl) Jackson Smith/Alamy Images. (br) LWA-Dan Tardif/ Corbis. (bkgd) Phototone Abstracts. Unit B Opener: Doug Perrine/Sea Pics. **A106–107** © Martin Harvey/Peter Arnold Inc. **B1** Jeff Jaskolski/Sea Pics. **B2–B3** (bkgd) J. Schultz /T. Soucek/AlaskaStock.com. **B3** (tr) George Ranalli/Photo Researchers, Inc. (c) Georgette Douwma/Photographer's Choice/Getty Images. (br) Karl Maslowski/Photo Researchers, Inc. **B4** (bl) Photonica. **B4–B5** (bkgd) Terry W. Eggers/Corbis. **B7** John Anderson/Animals Animals. **B8** (t) RGK Photography/Stone/Getty Images. (b) Jeff Foott/Bruce Coleman, Inc. **B9** (t) John Anderson/Animals Animals. (c) Jeff Foott/ Bruce Coleman, Inc. (b) RGK Photography/ Stone/Getty Images. **B10** (t) Lynda Richardson/Corbis. **B10–B11** (bkgd) Michael Fogden/DRK Photo. **B12** (bl) John Anderson/ Animals Animals. **B14** (t) Art Wolfe. (b) Jake Rajs/Stone/Getty Images. **B15** (b) Ralph Krubner/Index Stock Imagery, Inc. (t) Steve Dunwell/Index Stock Imagery, Inc. **B17** (c) Ralph Krubner/Index Stock Imagery, Inc. **B19** (tr) Tom and Pat Leeson/Photo Researchers, Inc. (bkgd) Galen Rowell/Corbis. **B20** (bl) Michael Fogden/DRK Photo. **B20–B21** (bkgd) © Dwight Kuhn Photography. **B22** P. Sharpe/ OSF/Animals Animals. **B23** (cl) Norbert Wu/ DRK Photo. (b) Warren Photographic. **B26** (bl) © E.R. Degginger/Color Pic, Inc. (br) Gregory K. Scott/Photo Researchers, Inc. **B27** (t) P. Sharpe/OSF/Animals Animals. (b) © E.R. Degginger/Color-Pic, Inc. **B32–B33** (bkgd) Ahup Shah/DRK Photo. **B33** (tc) George D. Lepp/Photo Researchers, Inc. (cr) R. Ian Lloyd/Masterfile. **B34–B35** J. Borris/Zefa/ Masterfile. **B38** (l) © E.R. Degginger/Color Pic, Inc. (r) Paul Sterry/Worldwide Picture Library/Alamy Images. **B39** (l) Konrad Wothe/Minden Pictures. (r) Jeremy Woodhouse/Pixelchrome.com. **B41** (c) Paul Sterry/Worldwide Picture Library/Alamy Images. **B42** (c) Esselte Corporation. **B42–43** (bkgd) Jason Stone/Leeson Photography. **B43** (tl) Bettmann/Corbis. (frame) Image Farm. **B44–B45** Mike Lane/Photo Researchers, Inc. **B46** Jack Wilburn/Animals Animals. **B47** (b) Nigel J Dennis/NHPA. (tr) Kenneth W. Fink/Photo Researchers, Inc. **B49** Donald Specker/Animals Animals. **B50** © Joseph Sohm/Visions of America/Corbis. **B51** (t) Mike Lane/Photo Researchers, Inc. **B56–B57** (bkgd) © Norbert Wu. **B57** (tr) David Cavagnaro/Peter Arnold, Inc. (br) © Jonathan Blair/Corbis. (c) Lloyd Cluff/Corbis. **B58** (bl) Anne DuPont. **B58–B59** (bkgd) Brandon D. Cole/Corbis. **B60** Sharon Cummings/Dembinsky Photo Associates. **B61** (bl) C.K. Lorenz/Photo Researchers, Inc. (br) John Eastcott/YVA Momatiuk/Photo Researchers, Inc. (tr) Michael Fogden/DRK Photo. (tl) Nigel J. Dennis; Gallo Images/ Corbis. **B62** (cr) Wayne Lankinen/DRK Photo.